HOW TO READ A NOVEL

Also by Caroline Gordon

NOVELS

The Malefactors
The Strange Children
The Women on the Porch
Green Centuries
The Garden of Adonis
None Shall Look Back
Aleck Maury
Penhally

SHORT STORIES

The Forest of the South

EDITED BY CAROLINE GORDON AND ALLEN TATE

The House of Fiction: An Anthology of the Short Story

HOW TO READ A NOVEL

by

Caroline Gordon

1958

THE VIKING PRESS, *Publishers*

FIRST PUBLISHED IN 1957
BY THE VIKING PRESS, INC.
625 MADISON AVENUE, NEW YORK 22

PUBLISHED IN CANADA
BY THE MACMILLAN COMPANY OF CANADA LIMITED
SECOND PRINTING 1958

LIBRARY OF CONGRESS CATALOG CARD NUMBER: 57-12613

PRINTED IN U.S.A. BY THE COLONIAL PRESS INC.

To Susan Jenkins Brown

Contents

CHAPTER		PAGE
1.	*How Not to Read a Novel*	3
2.	*The Novel as an Art Form*	14
3.	*Complication and Resolution*	26
4.	*The Scene of a Novel*	58
5.	*The Center of Vision*	72
6.	*The Effaced Narrator*	96
7.	*Henry James and His Critics*	111
8.	*The Central Intelligence*	120
9.	*Tone, Style, and Controlling Metaphor*	145
10.	*The Decline of the Hero*	171
11.	*The Novelist and His World*	192
12.	*Reading for Enjoyment*	220
	NOTES	235
	INDEX	241

HOW TO READ A NOVEL

Chapter One

How Not to Read a Novel

I have an aunt who disapproves of adultery. She does not hold with incest, either, or mayhem, rapine, or murder. Whenever I publish a novel I receive from her a letter whose contents seldom vary—a letter of stern rebuke, written, she maintains, in my best interests. She is convinced, she says, that I myself have never committed any of the crimes that occur so often and so lamentably in my novels, that I am, indeed, incapable of committing them. But how, she concludes plaintively, are other people to know that? As long as these crimes abound in my novels, people who do not know me personally are apt to form a poor opinion of my character. She usually ends by urging me to mend my ways.

My aunt's standard of behavior is that of a Southern lady of the old school. But she is no fool. If she places considerable emphasis on decorum it is because she knows it for what it is: the thin ice on which we all must skate as long and as skillfully as we can if we are not to fall into the abyss that yawns for each of us. One of my aunt's lifelong preoccupations has been peering into the abyss with an eye at once so sharp and so compassionate that it has on occasion excited my professional envy. After leaving a tea party she will, as it were, lift one corner of the veil long enough to point out cavernous depths as yet unplumbed by me, whose profession it is to explore human relationships. My aunt understands human relationships as well as the next one—perhaps better. *But she does not know how to read a novel.*

I have a friend—perhaps I had better say I *had* a friend, for by mutual agreement we do not see much of each other nowadays—who looks on the modern novel with an even more jaundiced eye than my aunt's. My aunt does not much care what goes on in a novel as long as people adhere to a certain moral code. My friend has other strictures. To begin with, she will not read a novel which has the word "black" in its title. She will not read, either, any novel in which children or animals are treated cruelly—that is, any contemporary novel. In her day, of course, she has read many a work in which both children and animals fared ill—from Dickens' *Oliver Twist* to Huysmans' account of the life and trial of Gilles de Rais. But these portrayals, she holds, belong in the past or, better still, in a foreign language. The contemporary novelist who writes of such goings on does so at the risk of her grave displeasure.

It was a love of dogs, not literature, that brought us together in the first place, and our friendship lasted several years—until I wrote a novel whose scenes are laid in East Tennessee in pioneer times. My novel followed the fortunes of a family which, "removing" from North Carolina to settle in the valley of the Holston, had incurred some of those misfortunes that ordinarily befell the early settlers in those parts. My friend told me that she had succeeded in reading the book only with great difficulty; she could not bear to think of children as being scalped or having their brains dashed out by Indians.

I did not promise to mend my ways. Instead I wrote another novel—as people so often do, once they get started. In this novel a horse was killed, a beautiful black stallion. My friend wrote me that this time she *could* not finish the book. Something told her that things were not going to turn out well for that horse, so she laid the book down almost as soon as she took it up.

One of these ladies whom I have mentioned was brought up in the provincial South. The other bears a name that is one of the most famous in the annals of New England. Each of them, being well past sixty, has had an advantage that is, for the most part, denied to the younger generation: a classical education. My aunt can still quote Horace. My New England friend once astonished a visiting classicist by capping the line he had just quoted from the Greek poet Callimachus. But you cannot accuse either of these ladies of living in the past. Like everybody else, they have had to change their ways to suit the times. My aunt, in her youth a daring horsewoman, now drives a motor car. And it is not in material things alone that these ladies have kept abreast of their times, for each of them leads a stirring intellectual life. My New England friend read Kierkegaard long before I did. My aunt is the only woman I know who reads Jakob Böhme; but she cannot "stand" Kafka or Joyce. And my New England friend says that she would not allow one of Faulkner's characters inside her house.

Their lines, as I have said, have fallen in different

places, but as far as fiction goes their tastes are identical. Each of them makes the same demands of a novel: that it be full of sweetness and not too much light. When I am annoyed by their naïve comments on contemporary fiction, I remind myself that each of these charming, intelligent ladies is, after all, a dilettante. The intellectual curiosity that impels them to read Kierkegaard or Whitehead somehow does not operate when they approach a contemporary novel. Their tastes in fiction were formed in the Victorian era, and they have not had occasion to change them.

At least this is what I used to tell myself—till one day I came upon some observations on the art of fiction which struck me as being fully as naïve as the strictures of my two charming ladies. These observations were made by a man who could in no sense be considered a dilettante. Indeed, he is considered—and rightly, I am sure—one of the greatest minds of modern times.

The "psychological" literary critics have made much of the "sibling rivalry" which they maintain must have existed between Henry James and his older brother William, the philosopher and pioneer psychologist. The evidence does not bear them out. The correspondence which Henry and William James kept up all their lives does not show that either of these great men cherished any feeling of envy or even of rivalry toward the other; their gifts were too dissimilar and each of them was too well aware of the character of his own gift to feel rivalry. Only once in their correspondence does one find them in serious disagreement.

William James once wrote his brother suggesting that

he try to write the kind of book that Finley Peter Dunne, who at that time was having a great popular success with his "Misther Dooley" pieces, was writing. Henry James replied that he would go dishonored to his grave if he wrote the kind of fiction that William liked to read.

This is a hard saying, but no harder, I think, than the case demands. William James was not only a man of the highest integrity but a man of enormous capabilities. He gave the best of himself to his work and in so doing revolutionized much of the thought of his times. In our own day his influence is not yet spent. I feel sure that he would have been appalled at the notion of passing a shoddy piece of work off as his own. Yet that, in effect, is what he is urging his brilliant younger brother to do, to stop writing the kind of book that only he could write and write the kind of book that had already proved itself popular—in short, to substitute imitation for genuine creation.

His suggestion was made with the best will in the world and made, certainly, in no venal spirit, and therefore, I think, could have sprung only from ignorance—not only of the particular technical problems his brother was facing, but of the processes by which a novel comes into being. Henry James' answer was made without rancor and is, in essence, a recognition of the profound gulf that yawns between the artist and his audience, a gulf, an abyss, that every performer spends his life trying to cross, as if upon a tightrope. Henry James, the novelist, knew what the great philosopher did not know—how tight a rope he himself had stretched, how fathomless the abyss that yawned beneath it.

But my two charmers are, after all, pushing seventy, and William James was born in 1842. I sometimes ask myself whether there is not, after all, something new under the sun. The times have changed in many ways; has the art of fiction changed with them? Certainly, some of the ways in which the times have changed have come to my professional attention. I was twenty-seven years old before I ever encountered another human being who was interested in the techniques of fiction. But nowadays almost every college campus has a fiction writer among its "artists in residence." An aspiring young writer who wants professional criticism of his work does not have to go far to get it. And the colleges and universities do even more than provide professional criticism of the tyro's work. They give a kind of encouragement which, I think, has never before been given to the budding artist. The struggles which used to go on in lonely garrets or basements, by the light of a taper or oil lamp, are now enacted in the classroom or lecture hall in the light of day—if not of klieg lights—attended, often, by a blare of publicity. There are actually institutions of learning in which an amateur writer can receive a bachelor's or master's degree for the writing of his first novel.

I know a young man—I will call him Y—who is taking a degree at one of our great universities and has chosen for the subject of his dissertation the work of a certain septuagenarian novelist whom I will call X. (He would like the label because of its associations with the mathematical formulae in which X figures as the "unknown quantity.") X has been publishing novels for many years but he maintains that his work is as yet unknown. His public appearances are characterized by an extraordinary degree of reticence, indeed of modesty, but sometimes, when speaking of his own work among trusted intimates, he has been known to emit a blast so loud that it seems calculated not only to awaken the illustrious dead but to topple over some gravestones. When it comes to contemporary fiction writers three remarks are often on his lips: "He won't do," "He'll do—as far as he goes," and "He hasn't read me yet." I myself suspect that X is right, in the main.

I did not try to bring X and Y together, but when they met at my house by accident, I was pleased. They got on well together, so well that I excused myself on the plea of some domestic duty and left them planning a visit Y was going to make to X's house—to look over the first draft of X's most famous novel. But Y never visited X and when I mentioned Y's name to X some months later he shook his ponderous head and said, "That boy won't do."

I reflected that as far as I could see Y's only fault lay in admiring X's work, perhaps inordinately. "You liked him well enough when you first met him," I said, not without malice.

X shook his head again. "He talks about the 'novel of ideas,' " he said. "He doesn't know that there isn't any such thing!"

My friendship with my New England friend came to grief because she felt that in my novels I countenance the scalping of children (though she knows quite well that I would not willingly scalp a worm). My friendship with Y came to the same kind of end. I do not see much of him these days. When he wanted to know why X had so abruptly changed his mind about inviting him to his house or even allowing him to see the first draft of that novel, I could say only, "It's because you talk about the novel of ideas." "But why?" he wanted to know. "Can't there be more than one kind of novel and one kind of novelist? Can't I admire X and Aldous Huxley, too?" "I'm afraid you can't," I had to tell him. At the time I couldn't furnish any cogent reason why these two admirations should be mutually exclusive, but I have been thinking of the matter, off and on now, for several years, and have come to certain conclusions which are, in a way, answers to the questions asked by the four readers I have mentioned.

For the convenience of my own readers, I will sum up these questions. (a) My aunt wants to know why the characters in my novels don't adhere to the moral code to which she adheres. (b) My New England friend wonders why, as a novelist, I persist in bringing unpleasant happenings to her attention when I could as easily portray pleasant happenings. (c) William James wanted to know why his brilliant younger brother could not employ his gifts in writing books that people liked to read instead of writing books that very few people wanted to read. (d) And Y, the student of the art of the novel, feels that it is just as permissible for a novel to concern itself with ideas as with action. It would be easy to say that my aunt and my learned New England friend—and the still more learned William James—did not know what they were talking about. I could even invoke weighty authority to sustain this viewpoint. The British philosopher R. G. Collingwood, in his valuable book, *The Principles of Art,* says that most of us don't know what we are talking about when we use the term "art." He says, "The thing which most constantly demands and receives the title of art is the thing whose real name is amusement or entertainment."

Collingwood maintains that the distinguishing feature of "amusement art" is that it is not "useful" in the way that "art proper" is. He says:

> An amusement is a device for the discharge of emotions in such a way that they shall not interfere with the concerns of practical life. . . . In order that emotion may be discharged without affecting practical life, a make-believe situation must be created in which to discharge it. This situation will of course be one which "represents" the real situation in which the emotion would discharge itself practically. The difference between the two, which has been indicated by calling them respectively real and make-believe, is simply this: the so-called make-believe situation is one in which it is understood that the emotion discharged shall be "earthed"; that is, that it shall not involve the consequences which it would involve under the conditions of practical life.

If I interpret Collingwood's thesis properly, the man who has spent the evening reading Sherlock Holmes in an easy chair, before a blazing fire, is not likely to act differently toward his fellow creatures the next morning, no matter how much he admires Sir Arthur Conan Doyle's masterly creation. On the other hand, the man who succeeds in finishing the reading of *War and Peace*—not everybody does—may not feel himself the same man afterward, and this change of heart may reflect itself so clearly in his daily conduct that other people will recognize the change.

This difference between "art proper" and "amusement art" has been recognized by two modern fiction writers. F. Scott Fitzgerald made such a sharp distinction in his own mind between his "amusement art" and his "art proper" that among his intimates he spoke of the stories he published in popular magazines as "sold down the river" and objected strenuously if his friends even referred to them. A contemporary novelist, Graham Greene, made the distinction more clearly and reasonably, when, some years ago, he labeled certain of his works as "entertainments."

The reader who is interested in this distinction would do well to read the argument between Plato and Aristotle concerning the nature of "art" and "representative art." (Collingwood, indeed, maintains that it is the misreading of what Plato has to say about art in the tenth book of the *Republic* that has caused much of the confusion in the modern world.[1] *)

But these are deep waters. Our present concern is with the general reader and what he demands of the novelist—and what the novelist, in turn, demands of him. The four readers I have mentioned are all highly individualistic, but I think that the questions they ask are questions that might well be asked by any serious, intelligent reader who did not happen to have special or technical training.

* See notes at end of book.

These questions all deal with one thing: the essential nature of fiction. Perhaps the reader must first find out what a novel *is* before he can read one intelligently and rewardingly. At any rate, the following chapters are attempts to answer two questions: "What is a novel?" and "How should it be read?"

Chapter Two

The Novel as an Art Form

What *is* a novel? The question is, indeed, more easily asked than answered. I have been writing fiction for twenty-five years but I would be hard put to it to define the essential nature of the novel as an art form. I can more readily say what it is not than what it is. Certainly the idea entertained by many people that a novel or even a short story is, as they say, a "slice of life" is all wrong. This notion appeals not only to the casual reader; many professional writers who are themselves highly gifted also hold to it. The late G. K. Chesterton, for instance, once remarked that there is no such thing as a novel by Charles Dickens, "but only something cut off from the vast and flowing stream of his personality."

Dickens, as a man, was what the psychiatrists would call "maladjusted." His conduct, particularly toward members of his family, was often more like that of a badly brought up adolescent than that of an adult, but he came very near to being a great novelist and is acknowledged by his peers as one of the greatest masters of certain techniques indispensable in the writing of fiction. To be specific: he excelled in what we call "scenic effects," that is, he could set his stage, people it, and put his characters in motion better than any of his contemporaries, a fact which

Thackeray often ruefully acknowledged. If Dickens were alive today, I imagine that the "stream of his personality" would flow like molten lava and might even erupt at the thought of his novels' not being works of art.

Chesterton is not alone in this delusion, however. Professor Howard Mumford Jones says of Sherwood Anderson:

> One can assert that there is no such thing as a work of fiction by Sherwood Anderson. The novels are autobiographical, the autobiographical books have in them the elements of fiction, the letters read like the first draft of a novel. There are short stories so compact that they might become novels, and there are novels that are at best only diluted short stories. Yet this library, at once unified and variegated, has its common denominator. The books represent facets of Sherwood Anderson's personality whose friends ranged from Gertrude Stein to the stoneworker near Ripshin farm in Virginia, and whose alternating moods of exaltation and despair are as kaleidoscopic as ever Byron's were.[2]

It seems to me that Professor Jones, in making this pronouncement, has failed to take into consideration the ineluctable fact that a novel is a work of art, and therefore subject to the laws of its own being, and not a facet of the author's personality, be he ever so Byronic, have he ever so many friends.

Sherwood Anderson's personality was, indeed, engaging, and he had alternating moods of exaltation and despair (like so many of us), but he was also a considerable artist. His work is certainly uneven. I myself do not feel that he ever succeeded in writing a real novel; his talent was pre-eminently for the short story, but he has left short stories behind him which are well-nigh flawless, and they are not "facets of his personality" but works of art, complete in themselves. "I Want to Know Why," "I'm a Fool," "The Triumph of the Egg" are contributions to literature, not autobiography.

That, at least, is the opinion of one author, although many professional writers would not agree with me. Why is there such a diversity of opinion among serious readers, and among authors themselves, as to the merits of various novels—indeed, as to the nature of the art form itself?

I suspect that it is because the novel is different from any other form of art. If we are to become good readers of fiction, we must learn to recognize and in our own minds define this essential difference. But perhaps we might set about defining it by first asking ourselves what the novel has in common with other art forms.

It has this in common with all art forms: it has a medium, and that medium, like all mediums, has limitations or boundaries. It is one of the primary tasks of the artist not only to recognize those boundaries but, on occasion, when his art demands it of him, to exceed them. A man coming into possession of a tract of land that proves to be larger than he had expected it to be might acknowledge this fact by extending the fence which encloses the field. So, any fiction writer who uses a method that has not been used before, or explores a method already in use more thoroughly than it has been explored hitherto, extends the boundaries of the medium. But we come back to a consideration of the nature of the medium itself. The French philosopher Jacques Maritain has put it better than anybody else, I think, when he says, in *Art and Scholasticism,*[1] that the novel differs from other forms of art in being directly concerned with the conduct of life itself.

This is doubtless one reason why there can be such a divergence of opinion, even among professional writers, as to what is a good novel or a bad novel, or even what is a novel and what isn't. It is the very nature of the medium, as complicated, as intractable, as mysterious as life itself, that makes for this confusion, a kind of confusion which does not reign in the other arts. I, for instance, do not know my notes and I have never, even for an instant, labored under the delusion that I could compose a piece of music. But I rarely meet a person who does not feel at the bottom of his heart that he could write a novel if he (half) tried. There is a good reason for this, of course. Everybody who is alive *knows* that he has in his own life the makings of a magnificent piece of fiction.[2] But these happenings, however moving and dramatic, are not in themselves fiction, but only the material out of which we may fashion fiction—if we have the talent and the time and the patience.

Malcolm Cowley has defined a novel as a "long but unified story, designed to be read at more than one sitting, that deals with the relations among a group of characters and leads to a change in those relations." The distinctions made by the philosopher Maritain and the critic Cowley seem to supplement each other. The novel is, indeed, different from other forms of art in that it concerns itself with the conduct of life, but it also concerns itself primarily with a change in those relations that make up the lives of a number of persons—if we adhere to Mr. Cowley's definition, which seems to me a good one. The primary concern of a novel, then, is life, and life as it manifests itself in change, in action.

But all life is, in a sense, change. From the moment we are born until the moment we die we are undergoing bodily and spiritual changes. Even if the author confines the "action" which is his story to twenty-four hours in the life of a person, as James Joyce did in *Ulysses,* he is still hard put to render everything that happened in the course of that action. In *Ulysses* Joyce seems to have come as close to it as is humanly possible, but there is still a great deal that he hasn't told us about the life of Mr. Bloom or Stephen Dedalus or Molly Bloom.

How does the artist go about fashioning fictions out of the intangible, mysterious stuff of life? What is the principle that guides him in deciding which events in a character's life are to be included in his story and which left out? And what is the unifying principle which binds all these incidents together to make the action that constitutes a novel? If we are to become good readers of fiction it behooves us to try to understand the nature of the process. I imagine that the solution to this particular problem can be arrived at—as the solutions of so many problems in life are arrived at—only by a kind of humility. In life we often have to give up one thing in order to get another. The reader who wants to read understandingly—whether he is reading *War and Peace* or the admirable detective stories of Raymond Chandler—must perform an act of self-abasement. He must lay aside his own opinions for the time being, and ask himself not why Mr. Chandler or Count Tolstoi didn't write the kind of book he would like to see them write, but what kind of book they have actually written. That is, he must try to understand what the fiction writer has accomplished before he allows himself to express an opinion on how—or why—he went about accomplishing it.

This practice, which is not at all popular in our public prints, is nevertheless salutary and indispensable for the proper reading of any fiction on any level. It is our way of collaborating with the author, a kind of collaboration which every author has the right to demand of every reader. By putting ourselves, as best we can, in his place, we share to some extent in the sacrifice he made in order to write his book and are therefore in a position to reap our share of the rewards of his work. To do this intelligently we must not only make an effort to put ourselves in the place of the author but actually try to follow in his footsteps.

At first glance, it would seem that the best way to do this is to find out what the author was trying to do when he wrote his book. But the author's intention is not always a reliable guide, and the reader who accepts it may be in danger of succumbing to what two modern critics have called the "Intentional Fallacy." Professors W. K. Wimsatt, Jr., and M. C. Beardsley, in an essay published in the *Sewanee Review* under that title, argue that "the design or intention of the author is neither available nor desirable as a standard for judging the success of a work of literary art." Support for this view may be found in the works of various authors. Proust, for instance, certainly did not succeed in doing all he set out to do in his magnificent long novel. On the other hand, authors sometimes accomplish something they did not have in mind. Dostoevski's original conception of *The Possessed* was a book which would be different from any other book he had written, a kind of thriller.

The intention of the author ought, of course, to be taken into consideration when we read his book, but with reservations. The work of art, once it is created, has an existence separate from that of its author, and "belongs now to the public," as Professors Wimsatt and Beardsley point out. Perhaps the safest way to follow in the author's footsteps is to try to understand some of the problems he confronted in writing his book. A writer's talent is God-given. I do not know any way under heaven by which a person who was not dowered with the gift for writing fiction at birth can acquire such a gift. But technique is another matter, and it is the duty of every fiction writer to acquire the techniques that will best serve his gifts. The foremost task that confronts the young fiction writer is to learn as much as he can about the secrets of his craft. There are people who would disagree with me about this. They would say that the foremost task of the young fiction writer is to write. The late Sinclair Lewis, when confronted with a class in creative writing, once asked, "So you want to write?" And when the members of the class replied en masse that they did, he replied, "Well, go home and write, then."

Never was worse advice given to young writers, as I know to my sorrow. (Some of the members of that class have asked me to read the "work" they produced after following his advice.) You don't "write" the way you breathe. You write *something:* a short story, a novel, an essay, an autobiography, a poem. Each of these has its different requirements. The fiction writer, the biographer, the essayist, even the author of the autobiography, each practices a craft that has its secrets, and the young writer—if he isn't born knowing them, as very few writers are— has to learn them. But how can he go about learning them?

As far as I can see there are only two ways. He can learn by trial and error, that is, by his own work. It is a slow and painful process, but one he had better not slight. As a rule, one must write a great many words before one learns to write well. There is another way, not a substitute for trial and error, but a path the author must take in the intervals when he is not writing—if he is not blinded by his own egotism, if he is not above doing what Tolstoi did once after he had finished a book. He sat down and read one of Turgenev's stories and said, "That is the way I ought to have done it." Thomas Wolfe did not follow Tolstoi's example, and perhaps that is one reason why so much of his work is becoming hard to read. On one occasion F. Scott Fitzgerald expressed admiration for Wolfe's writing but advised him to exercise more selectivity. "The novel of selected incidents," Fitzgerald wrote Wolfe, "has this to be said, that the great writer like Flaubert has consciously left out the stuff that Bill or Joe (in his case Zola) will come along and say presently. So Mme. Bovary becomes eternal while Zola already rocks with age." Wolfe answered him, "Flaubert me no Flauberts, Bovary me no Bovarys, Zola me no Zolas."

Percy Lubbock has called Henry James the "scholar of the novel," and James says that the "art of representation bristles with questions, the very terms of which are difficult to apply and appreciate. Therefore it is that experience has to organize, for convenience and cheer, some system of observation, for fear, in the admirable immensity, of losing one's way."

James' imagination was above all fictional, and his figure is rewarding when subjected to a closer analysis. The writing of a book *is* like a journey across an apparently trackless waste. We have the illusion that nobody else has ever left a footprint on those burning sands. Certainly we have to traverse the waste alone, and while we are in the act of traversing it we can't do much more than set one foot down after another; we can't listen to the voices of any of the travelers who have gone that way before, no matter how many admonitions and warnings they are calling out.

But one comes to the end of a journey and the day comes for almost every fiction writer when he finishes his book. He has been moving for months, sometimes for years, across that trackless waste, head down, hearing nothing but the sound of his own voice. But as soon as he reaches the other side he is assailed by a myriad of voices. His friends will repeat to him the things they have been saying for the last few months but which he hasn't heard very clearly, being wrapped up in his own thoughts. He hears them almost too clearly now! The members of his family have been storing up things to say to him, too. If he is married, his wife has visits she wants him to make, people she has been wanting to ask to dinner but couldn't for fear that they might arrive on an evening when he "felt like writing"; or she may hope that in the interim before he starts another book he will see more of the children, may even take Junior to the zoo. He may accompany Junior to the zoo and on the way answer all his questions with commendable patience, may spend several hours staring at the polar bears or watching the antics of the seals, but when he gets home he is likely to rush into his study and take down off the shelves a worn copy of *War and Peace* or *The Scarlet Letter* or *The Idiot*. While he was watching those seals gamboling other scenes rose before his mind's eye: a man, lying on his back on a bridge, staring up at the sky; a platform in the center of the marketplace in a colonial town and mounted on the platform a lank, black figure, ringed about with staring faces; or a railway station and a man standing transfixed by the look he has just received from a pair of burning eyes. He may have read *War and Peace* or *The Scarlet Letter* or *The Idiot* forty times before but he is suddenly seized with a strong desire to know how Tolstoi or Hawthorne or Dostoevski got a certain dramatic effect. He feels that if he reads the book one more time he may surprise the author in the act of creation, may divine his secret.

We can all learn from the masters, the men who have gone before us over that apparently trackless wilderness. If we follow faithfully enough in their footsteps we may find out something about them that will astonish us. A metaphor of Herman Melville so worked upon the imagination of a contemporary critic, Edmund Wilson, that he used it as the title for an anthology of critical essays: "For genius, all over the world, stands hand in hand, and one shock of recognition runs the whole circle round."

If we follow long and faithfully in the footsteps of the masters, I think we will participate in this "shock of recognition," will seem to see them meeting and greeting each other across the ages, almost as if they were members of the same band, of the same family.

We might extend Melville's figure further. If you observe the members of this band closely enough, passionately enough, you will not only find them stretching out their hands to each other across time and space but you will find that in all ages, in all places, they are *doing the same things.* It is as if artistic creation were a mighty dance, in which, upon appointed signals, the dancers perform certain steps, tread certain measures, with the paradoxical result that the dance, instead of crystallizing into a set form, becomes ever more unpredictable, more various, more glorious.

This is the "system of observation" which I have organized for myself, for fear of "losing my way" in the "admirable immensity" about which we have been talking. Painters speak of "constants" in painting. There are, I think, "constants" which you will find in all good fiction, from Sophocles and Aeschylus down to a well-constructed nursery tale. If one is going to write or read fiction, it is of paramount importance to be able to recognize these "constants" when one comes upon them, or, if they are not present in a work of fiction, to mark their absence.

And now let us return to the figure of the dancers. Those dancers are of all races, all ages, all conditions of servitude. Indeed, the stature of the artist seems to have little to do with the "shock of recognition." In this dance a giant may foot it featly with a pygmy and neither suffer any embarrassment. This was brought home to me very forcefully the other day when I was re-reading *Oedipus Rex* for perhaps the twentieth time. Once again I was admiring Sophocles' mastery of his material and his command of certain technical devices when my four-year-old granddaughter came into the room and asked me to read her Beatrix Potter's nursery tale, *Jemima Puddle-Duck.* I complied, and, somewhat to my surprise, found that Miss Potter was not only a master of her own medium but a master of some of the same technical devices which Sophocles used to such admirable effect in *Oedipus Rex.* Her little tale is full of them. Her heroine is a duck and Sophocles' legendary hero is a king but they have some of the same characteristics and confront some of the same problems. An examination of the work of the pygmy—I do not think that Miss Potter would have objected to being called a pygmy in this case—throws some light on the work of the giant. I will consider these two fictions in the next chapter, for they have much in common.

Chapter Three

Complication and Resolution

I

We all know the story of Oedipus: he grew up thinking that he was the son of the king and queen of Corinth and after the Delphic oracle told him that he would kill his father and marry his mother and bring disaster on his native city he left home to escape such a fate. On his wanderings he came to a crossroads where an old man in a mule-drawn car disputed his right of way. Oedipus killed him and, proceeding farther along one of the crossroads, came upon the Sphinx, the monster with the head of a woman and the body of a beast which lay outside the gates of Thebes and killed every passer-by who could not answer the question that every schoolboy nowadays can answer: What is it goes on four legs in the morning, two at noon, and three in the evening? But Oedipus was the first man to answer it and the grateful city rewarded him by giving him the hand of the recently widowed queen in marriage and making him its king. The story is a part of our heritage.

R. G. Collingwood has spoken of Aristotle's *Poetics* as being, in part, "a set of hints to amateur playwrights." The "pointers" that Aristotle gives the playwright in the course of his analysis of *Oedipus Rex* are equally valuable to serious readers of fiction. What he says about the play as an art form is equally true of the novel. Certainly his definition of a play as the imitation of an action of a certain magnitude[1] might be used to define the novel as an art form: not life—or even a slice of it—but the contrivance of an illusion of life as viewed during the course of some one event.

The action of *Oedipus Rex* falls, as Aristotle says every action falls, into two parts: Complication and Resolution. "By Complication," Aristotle says, "I mean all from the beginning of the story to the point just before the change in the hero's fortunes. By Resolution [I mean] the beginning of the change to the end." It would be good practice for every serious student of literature to form the habit of trying to resolve every piece of fiction he reads into these component parts.

It is not easy to do. A play, a fiction, does not fall into its two component parts the way an orange or apple does when halved. The parts are apparently inextricably mingled, and one of them masquerades as the other. But in any masterpiece the Resolution is always embedded in the Complication from the very start. The ideal effect, of course, is that in which the Resolution appears to grow out of the Complication as inevitably, as naturally, as a plant grows from a seed. The vital elements which will make the plant are not visible to the naked eye, but a botanist can discern them.

The action of *Oedipus Rex* is firmly rooted in the natural order, but the theme also has a supernatural connotation, one that was dear to the heart of the Greeks: *hubris,* which comes from the Greek verb *hubridzo,* to run riot—in short, man setting himself up against the established order, man in conflict with the gods. The note of the supernatural is struck from the first, even in the stage setting. The action takes place on the platform before the king's palace because the king is the protagonist. What is a protagonist? A man who struggles. What or whom is the king struggling against? The gods. Therefore there are altars at the right and left of the platform, and suppliants, people who are praying to the gods to deliver the city from the plague, lie on the steps in attitudes of despair. There are three steps leading down from the platform into the "orchestra" or chorus-ground. This is fitting. The chorus and the suppliants both represent the world. The suppliants can only suffer; the chorus leader, speaking for the chorus, has the capacity not only to suffer but to extract wisdom from his suffering. At the end of the play, he has, so to speak, changed his tune. But his first speech and his last speech have this in common: both strike the note of the supernatural.

Oedipus comes out of his palace, sees the suppliants lying on the steps of the altars, and says:[2]

> My children, generations of the living
> In the line of Kadmos, nursed at his ancient hearth:
> Why have you strewn yourselves before these altars
> In supplication, with your boughs and garlands?
> The breath of incense rises from the city
> With a sound of prayer and lamentation. Children,

I would not have you speak through messengers,
And therefore I have come myself to hear you—
I, Oedipus, who bear the famous name.

The whole action is set in train in this first speech. Oedipus is not going to delegate authority. He has come himself to help his people, but one reason he is so ready to help them is that he is conscious that he is no ordinary man, but Oedipus, who bears the famous name.

The priest underlines Oedipus' *hubris* in his opening speech when he says:

You are not one of the immortal gods, we know;
Yet we have come to you to make our prayer
As to the man of all men best in adversity
And wisest in the ways of God. You saved us
From the Sphinx, that flinty singer, and the tribute
We paid to her so long; yet you were never
Better informed than we, nor could we teach you:
It was some god breathed in you to set us free.

Therefore, O mighty King, we turn to you:
Find us our safety, find us a remedy,
Whether by counsel of the gods or men. . . .

Even while the priest is telling Oedipus that he knows he is not a god, he is reminding Oedipus and the people too that Oedipus has already been a victor in a contest with the supernatural, when he vanquished the Sphinx, who, having the head of a woman and the body of a beast, did not belong to the natural order. The Complication is thus set forth in the first few speeches and immediately afterward the author foreshadows the Resolution. But he does it in such a way that our conscious minds do not recognize it for what it is.

There are various ways of accomplishing this technical feat. Sometimes it is done onomatopoetically, that is, by the very sound of the words. A famous example is the first sentence in Edgar Allan Poe's "The Fall of the House of Usher":

> During the whole of a dull, dark, and soundless day in the autumn of the year, when the clouds hung oppressively low in the heavens, I had been passing alone, on horseback, through a singularly dreary tract of country; and at length found myself, as the shades of evening drew on, within view of the melancholy House of Usher.

The very sound of those syllables bodes no good. We are not surprised when the House of Usher falls into the deep and dank tarn which Poe has so carefully prepared for its reception.

Ordinarily, the Resolution is introduced into the Complication disguised—that is, disguised as part of the action. This is Sophocles' method, but he gives it a further twist by presenting it to us in reverse. The priest says to Oedipus:

> Ah, when your years of kingship are remembered,
> Let them not say *We rose, but later fell. . . .*

That is exactly what they are going to say, what the priest, himself, as leader of the chorus, is going to say, but since he puts the speech into the form of a warning rather than a prophecy we fail, if we don't know the myth, to recognize it for what it is and accept it as part of the Complication rather than part of the Resolution.

And now, putting aside, for the moment, this great principle which one might spend a lifetime in mastering, let us turn our attention to the hinge, as it were, upon which these two parts of the action turn, to what Aristotle calls "Discovery," defining it as the "change from ignorance to knowledge, and thus to either love or hate, in the personages marked for either good or evil fortune." Oedipus is marked for evil fortune, so his loves are fated to turn into hate. He can no longer love his wife in the way he has loved her, and his very paternal affection is curdled, since his children are, as he puts it, conceived in the same bed in which he was conceived. He has been guilty of a good deal of self-love, but at the end of the play he can no longer even love himself, for he is the man who brought these misfortunes not only on the heads of those he loved but also on his own head.

Our task now is to ascertain what methods Sophocles uses to bring about this great reversal of fortune, this change from ignorance to knowledge, from love to hate. There is one technical device that stands him in good stead: the Peripety. Aristotle has defined it as

> the change from one state of things in the play to its opposite of the kind described, and that too in the way we are saying, in the probable or necessary sequence of events; as it is for instance in *Oedipus:* here the opposite

> state of things is produced by the Messenger, who, coming to gladden Oedipus and to remove his fears as to his mother, reveals the secret of his birth.

The adjectives "probable" and "necessary" are very important here. It is excellent if the Peripety comes about in the "probable sequence of events," but it is still better when it seems to come about through a "necessary sequence of events." We sometimes use the word "inevitable" in describing such a Peripety. When we do that we pay an author one of the highest compliments. We mean that he has contrived such a completely lifelike illusion that for the moment we are deceived into taking it for life itself.

Let us examine this technical device, this Peripety, which for centuries has excited the admiration of serious students of literature. It's a little like the old shell-and-pea game at the county fair. The operator makes you think he is doing one thing when all the time he is doing something else, and he uses one hand to conceal the movements of the other. Sophocles tells us one thing and our conscious minds accept it as a fact, but all the time the unconscious mind to which he is also addressing himself is giving a different interpretation or sometimes adding another interpretation. We call this irony. Fowler, in his *Dictionary of Modern English Usage,* defines irony as "a form of utterance that postulates a double audience." The irony of the Greek drama, he says, "had the peculiarity of providing a double audience—one party in the secret and one party not. . . . The characters were in the dark;

one of them might utter words that to him and his companions on the stage were of trifling import, but to those who hearing could understand were pregnant with the coming doom." We find an example of this kind of irony in Oedipus' first speech when he says he would not have his people speak through messengers. You can be sure he wouldn't—if he knew what was coming, knew that a messenger was already on the way, with the news of his own doom!

There is a peculiar pleasure in knowing more than a man who is as great as Oedipus. The dramatic ironies with which the play abounds add luster to the action. In his second speech Oedipus says:

> Poor children! . . .
> I know that you are deathly sick; and yet,
> Sick as you are, not one is as sick as I. . . .

Again, he is speaking the truth without knowing it.

When Creon comes back from his pilgrimage to the Delphic oracle and tells Oedipus and the chorus that it was "murder brought the plague-wind" and that Apollo has decreed that the murderer of Laius must be found and driven out of the city, Oedipus makes a speech that is even more ironic than those he has just made, for in it he pronounces judgment on himself:

> I solemnly forbid the people of this country,
> Where power and throne are mine, ever to receive that man
> Or speak to him, no matter who he is. . . .

> Whether it be a lurking thief, or one of a number—
> I pray that that man's life be consumed in evil and
> wretchedness.
> And as for me, this curse applies no less
> If it should turn out that the culprit is my guest here,
> Sharing my hearth.

In a speech just before this one Oedipus has asked Creon why the Thebans did not hunt down Laius' murderer soon after the crime was committed. Creon replies:

> The riddling Sphinx' song
> Made us deaf to all mysteries but her own.

These words apply to Oedipus just as much as to the Thebans. If Oedipus did not so pride himself upon having solved the riddle of the Sphinx, he might be better at solving the riddle that confronts him now, but he is swollen with pride and, blinded by self-esteem, is even blinder than the old seer, Tiresias, who is now led in by a boy. Tiresias, as a young man, caught sight of Diana and her nymphs bathing in a woodland pool and consequently was deprived of his eyesight, but he was given the gift of second sight to mitigate his punishment. He tells Oedipus that he, Oedipus, is the murderer of whom the oracle speaks, but Oedipus refuses to believe him and says:

> Could I have told . . .
> You'd come here to make a fool of yourself, and of me?

The whole interchange between Oedipus and Tiresias bristles with dramatic irony. Oedipus tells Tiresias to go and leave them in peace. "While you are here we can do nothing."

Tiresias says:

I will go when I have said what I have to say.
How can you hurt me? And I tell you again:
The man you have been looking for all this time,
The damned man, the murderer of Laïos,
That man is in Thebes. To your mind he is foreign-born,
But it will soon be shown that he is a Theban,
A revelation that will fail to please. A blind man
Who has his eyes now; a penniless man, who is rich now;
And he will go tapping the strange earth with his staff.
To the children with whom he lives now he will be
Brother and father—the very same; to her
Who bore him, son and husband—the very same
Who came to his father's bed, wet with his father's blood.

And then Tiresias makes one of the finest exits ever made from any stage.

In the next scene Complication turns into Resolution, for the hero's fortunes begin to change the moment Jocasta comes on the stage. Her very entrance is an example of dramatic irony. Oedipus has come to the conclusion that Creon is plotting against him in an attempt to usurp the throne and is using Tiresias as a cat's paw; it is easier for him to believe that his brother-in-law is a traitor than that he himself is a murderer. The leader of the chorus cuts the quarrel between Creon and Oedipus short and also predicts the part Jocasta is going to play in the action when he says:

> Now, my lords, be still. I see the Queen
> Iocastê, coming from her palace chambers.

Tradition assigns woman the role of peacemaker—not that she always fills it. Jocasta, trying hard to make peace, succeeds in bringing the house down on their heads. When Oedipus tells her that Creon has brought in "that damnable soothsayer" in an effort to prove that he, Oedipus, is the murderer, she reassures him. One cannot believe soothsayers; she herself has had experience with them:

> An oracle was reported to Laïos once . . .
> That his doom would be at the hands of his own son—
> His son, born of his flesh and of mine!

The soothsayer was proved wrong, she says:

> . . . Laïos was killed
> By marauding strangers where three highways meet;
> But his child had not been three days in this world
> Before the king had pierced the baby's ankles
> And had left him to die on a lonely mountain.
> Thus, Apollo never caused that child
> To kill his father, and it was not Laïos' fate
> To die at the hands of his own son, as he had feared.
> This is what prophets and prophecies are worth!
> Have no fear of them.

Her speech has exactly the opposite effect on Oedipus from what she intended. He says:

> How strange a shadowy memory crossed my mind,
> Just now while you were speaking; it chilled my heart.

That chilling of the heart marks the stirring in his unconscious mind of the memory which will change into Discovery when it has risen fully to the surface. He then begins to question Jocasta as to the circumstances of Laius' death, and when she tells him that Laius was killed at a place where three highways meet, memory stirs even more ominously. He asks her if the King was "lightly escorted, or did he ride with a large company, as a ruler should?"

Iocastê

> There were five men with him in all: one was a herald;
> And a single chariot, which he was driving.

Oedipus

> Alas, that makes it plain enough! but who—
> Who told you how it happened?

Iocastê

> A household servant,
> The only one to escape.

Oedipus

> And is he still
> A servant of ours?

Iocastê

No, for when he came back at last
And found you enthroned in the place of the dead king,
He came to me, touched my hand with his, and begged
That I would send him away to the frontier district
Where only the shepherds go—
As far away from the city as I could send him.
I granted his prayer; for although the man was a slave,
He had earned more than this favor at my hands.

Oedipus

Can he be called back quickly?

Iocastê

Easily. But why?

Oedipus

I have taken too much upon myself
Without enquiry; therefore I wish to consult him.

Iocastê

Then he shall come. But am I not one also
To whom you might confide these fears of yours?

Oedipus

That is your right; it will not be denied you.

Then he utters the wonderful speech in which he rehearses what he knows of his history and origins.

Polybos of Corinth is my father,
My mother is a Dorian, Meropê . . .

And I myself
Pronounced this malediction upon myself!

Chorus

We too, my lord, have felt dismay at this.
But there is hope: you have yet to hear the shepherd.

Oedipus

Indeed, I fear no other hope is left me.

Iocastê

What do you hope from him when he comes?

Oedipus

This much:
If his account of the murder tallies with yours,
Then I am cleared.

Iocastê

What was it that I said
Of such importance?

Oedipus

Why, "marauders," you said,
Killed the King, according to this man's story.
If he maintains that still, if there were several,
Clearly the guilt is not mine: I was alone.
But if he says one man, singlehanded, did it,
Then the evidence all points to me.

But Jocasta stands her ground.

The whole city heard it as plainly as I.
But suppose he alters some detail of it:
He can not ever show that Laïos' death
Fulfilled the oracle: for Apollo said
My child was doomed to kill him; and my child—
Poor baby!—it was my child that died first.

No. From now on, where oracles are concerned,
I would not waste a second thought on any.

Oedipus agrees that she may be right but insists that the shepherd be sent for.

And now comes the fortuitous event, the thing that was not foreseen but is yet so probable that we have no difficulty in accepting it. A messenger comes from Corinth to announce that Oedipus' reputed father, King Polybus, is dead. Jocasta is jubilant; her lack of faith in soothsayers is finding further confirmation.

Oedipus' spirits rise, too:

Ah!
Why should a man respect the Pythian hearth, or
Give heed to the birds that jangle above his head?
They prophesied that I should kill Polybos,
Kill my own father, but he is dead and buried.
And I am here—I never touched him, never,
Unless he died of grief for my departure,
And thus, in a sense, through me. No. Polybos
Has packed the oracles off with him underground.

They have their moments of *hubris* in which both he and Jocasta defy the gods, then Oedipus again has the chilling thought that his mother is still alive: "And yet —must I not fear my mother's bed?"

Jocasta reassures him:

Have no more fear of sleeping with your mother:
How many men, in dreams, have lain with their mothers!
No reasonable man is troubled by such things.

But the messenger from Corinth asks curiously, "Tell me, who is this woman that you fear?" And Oedipus replies that it is Merope, wife of King Polybus. The messenger then reveals to Oedipus that Polybus was not his father nor Merope his mother.

Oedipus

Then why did he call me son?

Messenger

I will tell you:
Long ago he had you from my hands, as a gift. . . .
I came upon you in the crooked pass of Kithairon.

Oedipus

And what were you doing there?

Messenger

Tending my flocks.

Oedipus

A wandering shepherd?

Messenger

But your savior, son, that day.
. . . Your ankles should tell you that.

Oedipus

Ah, stranger, why do you speak of that childhood pain?

Messenger

I cut the bonds that tied your ankles together.

Oedipus

I have had the mark as long as I can remember.

Messenger

That was why you were given the name you bear.

Oedipus

God! Was it my father or my mother who did it?

Messenger

I do not know. The man who gave you to me
Can tell you better than I.

Oedipus

It was not you who found me but another?

Messenger

It was another shepherd gave you to me.

Oedipus

Who was he? Can you tell me who he was?

Messenger

I think he was said to be one of Laïos' people.

Oedipus

You mean the Laïos who was king here long ago?

Messenger

Yes; King Laïos; and the man who was one of his herdsmen.

Oedipus

Is he still alive? Can I see him?

Messenger

These men here
Know best about such things.

The leader of the chorus here intervenes fatefully and says:

I think the man he means is that same shepherd
You have already asked to see. Iocastê perhaps
Could tell you something.

Jocasta says wildly, "Why think of him? Forget this herdsman. Forget it all. This talk is a waste of time."

But Oedipus now displays the spirit she has all along been urging him to have and says, "How can you say that, when the clues to my true birth are in my hands?"

He is Oedipus, who, even though he was handicapped from birth, having his feet pierced through with a thong when he was but an infant, will yet stand up on those swollen feet, from which he gets his name, and defy the gods.

Jocasta throws overboard the philosophy of life that she doubtless got from Oedipus and says, "For God's love, let us have no more questioning!"

But Oedipus will not give in. And he now makes the same mistake about Jocasta that he made about Creon, ascribing worldly motives to her, false pride. He says:

> You need not worry. Suppose my mother a slave,
> And born of slaves: no baseness can touch you.

And when she still begs him to leave off questioning he says:

> Go, one of you, and bring the shepherd here.
> Let us leave this woman to brag of her royal name.

To which Jocasta returns:

> Ah, miserable!
> That is the only word I have for you now.
> That is the only word I can ever have.

And, having brought about the change in fortune which the Chorus predicted she would bring about, she leaves the stage.

In the next scene the Shepherd is brought in to confront the Messenger from Corinth.

Oedipus

Did you give this man the child he speaks of?

Shepherd

I did.

And I would to God I had died that very day.

Oedipus

Where did you get him? From your house? From somewhere else?

Shepherd

. . . They said it was Laïos' child;

But it is your wife who can tell you about that.

Oedipus

My wife?—Did she give it to you?

Shepherd

My lord, she did.

Oedipus

Do you know why?

Shepherd

I was told to get rid of it.

Oedipus

An unspeakable mother!

Shepherd

There had been prophecies . . .

Oedipus

Tell me.

Shepherd

It was said that the boy would kill his own father.

Oedipus

Then why did you give him over to this old man?

Shepherd

I pitied the baby, my King,
And I thought that this man would take him far away
To his own country.—He saved him—but for what a fate!
For if you are what this man says you are,
No man living is more wretched than Oedipus.

Oedipus

Ah God! It was true! All the prophecies!—Now,
O Light, may I look on you for the last time!
I, Oedipus,
Oedipus, damned in his birth, in his marriage damned,
Damned in the blood he shed with his own hand!

He rushes into the palace and, when he finds that Jocasta is dead, blinds himself with a brooch torn from her gown. When he next comes on the stage he appears as Tiresias has prophesied that he would appear: as a blind man who will go "tapping the strange earth with his staff." It will be a strange earth, for Creon, who now rules, has decreed that Oedipus can no longer stay in Thebes for fear of contaminating the city by his very presence. The reversal is thus complete. The king has turned into the beggar, and the man who saw through everything—without the help of "birds that jangle above his head"—is now as blind as the soothsayer whom he mocked at the beginning of the play for having to depend on divination rather than his own eyes. The chorus, which at the beginning hailed him as the man best in adversity and wisest in the ways of God, now chants directly to the audience:

> Men of Thebes, look upon Oedipus.
> This is the king who solved the famous riddle
> And towered up, most powerful of men.
> No mortal eyes but looked on him with envy,
> Yet in the end ruin swept over him.
> Let every man in mankind's frailty
> Consider his last day; and let none
> Presume on his good fortune until he find
> Life, at his death, a memory without pain.

It is as if a great wheel revolved inside the play, or as if the hands of some giant clock moved slowly and what was noon becomes midnight as, indeed, it soon is for Oedipus.

But how has Sophocles accomplished this seemingly miraculous effect? How has he contrived "an imitation of life" more lifelike than any of his fellows' achievements? I think it is by so ordering his imitation of life that it corresponds to a picture implicit in the human imagination. In life things don't just happen. They are led up to by other events. There is always more than one sequence of events, and they cross and recross each other until the threads which make up the skein of any one person's fate seem, at least to mortal eyes, inextricably tangled. But now and then a man comes along and with what seems almost superhuman insight and endurance succeeds not only in unraveling the skein but in fashioning it into a similitude of life. This play has the sheen, the sparkle, of life but it also has the density, the unpredictability. If we examine the structure closely enough we perceive that it is one of the most complex fabrications ever produced by the human imagination. That is because it imitates life so closely. The events excite our interest, we are convinced that things happened the way Sophocles says they happened, but one reason we believe it is that he doesn't give us a chance to believe anything else. Everything that happens in this play is not only presented in a way that gives us the illusion of life but is prepared for in the way life prepares its effects: by the events that have gone before. And this difficult technical feat is accomplished not once or twice in the action of the play but is being accomplished in every scene, almost in every speech. Everything that happens is related to everything else that has happened and foreshadows what is going to happen. Every incident therefore has a threefold existence: in the past, the present, and the future.

A few writers have been able to achieve this effect in a small compass, or in certain passages of longer works, but no one else has achieved it on as grand a scale as Sophocles and with such completeness, such thoroughness. Perfect form—or what approaches perfect form—is rare in this world. I don't know just how one can go about attaining it. I suspect, however, that we have more chance of attaining it in our own work if we learn to recognize it when we see it in the works of others. And I think that any one who aspires to read fiction seriously cannot do better than contemplate the myriad technical excellences of this play. There is matter in it for a lifetime's contemplation.

II

Oedipus is a legendary hero and Jemima is only a duck, but they have one thing in common: a dissatisfaction with their condition, Oedipus with his human condition, Jemima with her duckly condition. Sophocles' great play is conceived so loftily and executed so brilliantly, with such a multiplicity of inventions, that we are dazzled by it. But Miss Potter shows herself master of some of the same technical devices that Sophocles used and she too has remarkable capacities for invention. Her nursery tale opens with a remark delivered by the omniscient narrator, which serves somewhat the same purpose as the chorus in Oedipus, a comment on the duckly rather than the human condition: "What a funny sight it is to see a brood of ducklings with a hen!"

In the next sentence the heroine is introduced: "Listen to the story of Jemima Puddle-Duck, who was annoyed because the farmer's wife would not let her hatch her own eggs."

It is the immemorial custom—at least it was before

the invention of the incubator—to put duck eggs under hens to be hatched. Hens are, somehow, better sitters. But Jemima Puddle-Duck wants to go against the established order and hatch her own eggs. Her sister-in-law, Mrs. Rebecca Puddle-Duck, who in the nursery tale has somewhat the same role that Creon has in *Oedipus Rex,* having a firmer grasp on reality than her gifted sister-in-law—Mrs. Rebecca Puddle-Duck says that if she herself has not the patience to sit on eggs for twenty-eight days, how can a flighty creature like Jemima hope to succeed in such an endeavor? (Trust an in-law to put her finger on your weakness!) Jemima, however, pays no more attention to her than Oedipus paid to Creon, and quacks only of her desires: "I wish to hatch my own eggs; I will hatch them all by myself." And, like Oedipus, she flies the coop—that is, she determines to leave the world she knows, the farm, and make herself a nest somewhere else.

Oedipus would have been all right if his temperament had allowed him to stay put, that is, if he had never left Corinth. But his anger at the drunken man who implies that he is not King Polybus' son is so great that he is impelled to action and, leaving Corinth in order that the Delphic oracle's prophecy may not come true, succeeds only in bringing it about.

Jemima leaves the farm with as much precipitancy, even flying part of the way. "The open place in the middle of the wood, where the trees and brushwood had been cleared away," seems a fine place for the fulfillment of her wishes when she first comes upon it, just as Thebes seemed a fine place to Oedipus—particularly when his *hubris,* his reliance on his own powers, is rewarded by his receiving the hand of the queen in marriage and becoming the king. But Fate, in letting him tower up, "most powerful of men," for a period of years, was only playing a cat-and-mouse game with him. He thinks that he has left Corinth behind. "Corinth," he says, "to me was only in the stars descending in that quarter of the sky," but he has not been able to destroy Corinth by leaving it. It is there all along, keeping his dreadful secret until the moment Fate ordains for it to be revealed.

The Sphinx whom he vanquished may be thought of as the instrument of his destruction; it is the pride and vainglory he feels on account of having been the only man to answer her riddle that makes him defy the gods in the person of the old soothsayer, "the old man . . . skilled at hearing Fate in the wing-beat of a bird." But Oedipus says, "Your birds—what good were they? or the gods, for the matter of that? But I came by, Oedipus, the simple man, who knows nothing—I thought it out for myself, no birds helped me!" And again: "Why should a man respect the Pythian hearth, or give heed to the birds that jangle above his head?"

The use of the word "birds" is ironic, since it is the old soothsayer, the man skilled in divination by means of the flight of birds, who brings about Oedipus' doom—and Oedipus would have done better to respect him. The Greek tragedians achieved some of their most dramatic effects by the use of irony, that is, the appeal to the "double audience," to the audience who, being acquainted with the myth on which the play is founded, already knows or suspects what the hero has yet to learn. Miss Potter relies almost as much on irony for her dramatic effects.

The first sight of the gentleman with the black pricked-up ears and sandy whiskers and the long bushy tail tells us, the audience, what kind of fellow he is. But Jemima thinks only that he is well dressed. She feels that such a handsome gentleman must surely be sympathetic, too, and at once begins telling him her troubles, how they give all the eggs she lays to a hen to be hatched, instead of letting her hatch them herself.

The sandy-whiskered gentleman says, "Indeed. How interesting! I wish I could meet up with that fowl. I would teach it to mind its own business."

We all know what he thinks a fowl's proper business is: to be eaten by a fox. But Jemima, blinded like Oedipus by self-interest and self-esteem, can't see what is going on around her—not even when the sandy-whiskered gentleman leads her into a wood-shed that is full of feathers. It does not occur to her that these feathers were probably plucked from some of her friends and relatives, though she *is* surprised at the softness and profusion of them. Oedipus had it soft, too, for a while after he vanquished the Sphinx.

We come now to the point where Complication turns into Resolution. Miss Potter, like all expert fiction writers, prepares a long time ahead for her dénouement. Jemima, looking for "a convenient, dry nesting place," picks out a stump that is surrounded by foxgloves. The very word "fox" tells the reader what is to come, and there is further preparation in the ironic interchanges between Jemima and the hospitable gentleman, as when he tells her he loves eggs and ducklings and would be proud to have a woodshed full of them. But Miss Potter knows that one cannot rely on the perspicacity of infants any more than on that of adults. She knows that she has to make her points in divers ways. At the crucial point, where Complication turns into Resolution, she does what many a great writer has done before her: she shifts her viewpoint from that of the third-person narrator back to that of the omniscient narrator, who sees all and knows all. Jemima finally succeeds in laying nine eggs. "They were greenish white and very large," says the omniscient narrator. "The foxy gentleman"—as the omniscient narrator now openly calls him—"admired them immensely. He used to turn them over and count them when Jemima was not there."

The Resolution—the change in the heroine's fortunes—proceeds with a rush once Jemima has laid thirteen eggs. Here we have the most dramatic of the dramatic ironies with which this little tale abounds. The climax is led up to by a beautiful piece of preparation. Jemima is made to fatten herself for the kill! The foxy gentleman tells her that he wants to give her a treat before she begins sitting—a dinner party, all to themselves—and he sends Jemima over to the farm to pluck sage, thyme, onions, all the herbs that go to make a savory stuffing for roast duck—all but the lard. "I will provide the lard," said the hospitable gentleman with the sandy whiskers and long bushy tail, for, as every housewife knows, there is a lot of grease to a duck.

Now comes on the stage the character who, playing somewhat the same part that the Messenger from Corinth plays in Oedipus, resolves the plot. Kep, the old, wise, kind collie, has observed Jemima's antics and asks her bluntly where she goes every day. Jemima, though a simpleton, is in awe of properly constituted authority—a trait that saves her life in the end. She tells him the whole story. He cannot help grinning when she describes the polite gentleman with the sandy whiskers and long bushy tail, who has a woodshed full of feathers, and after he has found out exactly where this woodshed is he trots off to the village in search, we might say, of the police.

Jemima returns to the woodshed and from now on we have the increased tempo that marks a certain stage of the Resolution. The sandy-whiskered gentleman jumps up from his log the moment she appears, takes the herbs from her, and tells her to get into the woodshed, addressing her so abruptly that she looks at him in surprise.

But she obeys and goes into the woodshed. A few minutes later Kep arrives with the foxhound puppies, and the kill—the death—takes place off-stage, as it does in a Greek tragedy. We hear "awful noises—barking, baying, growls and howls, squealing and groans," and "nothing more was ever seen of that foxy-whiskered gentleman." However, we are convinced, by what Henry James would call "strong specification," that a struggle to the death has taken place: Kep has a bite on one ear and both the puppies are limping.

Jemima seems to have suffered less damage than any of them. She is in tears and has lost that sitting of eggs, for the puppies rushed in and gobbled them up before Kep could stop them, but we know that Jemima will live to sit another day. She lays more eggs in June and this time —no doubt the gods have so decreed it in order that she may come to a full realization of her *hubris*—this time she is permitted to keep the eggs, but only four of them hatch. A duck followed by a whole flock of ducklings is a pretty, an imposing, sight, but a duck who has only four ducklings does not cut much of a figure in the barnyard. This is Jemima's punishment, her fate which she has rushed upon, by leaving the barnyard, by fleeing the scene of her duckly limitations.

"Jemima Puddle-Duck said that it was because of her nerves; but she had always been a bad sitter."

The last sentence, like the chorus in *Oedipus,* points the moral. It also serves to unify the action. At the end of the story Jemima is back where she started—in the barnyard. The setting, laid in with a few deft touches, is important in the action. Jemima's adventure has for its background the barnyard where ducks waddle about, cows stand waiting to be milked, hens sit patiently on their own eggs or duck eggs, and Kep, the wise old collie, keeps all in order. If Kep had been less wise, less all-seeing, the other ducks more rebellious, the barnyard itself less ordered, Jemima might never have fled to the grove of foxgloves. It is her reaction against the homely order of the barnyard which involves her with the sandy-whiskered gentleman with the black pricked-up ears.

If we do not know *where* something happened we will never be sure that it *did* happen—a psychological fact which the Greek tragedians took into account when they included among their three unities the unity of place, the two other unities being those of time and action.

In the beginning the Greek tragedians observed these unities faithfully. In the plays of Aeschylus and Sophocles events happen in a certain place and within a limited time. The unity of action also carried with it certain restrictions; acts of violence, for instance, took place off the stage, whence comes the derivation of the word "obscene"—literally, off-stage. Euripides, impelled by a spirit which, even after the lapse of all these centuries, one can only describe as "modern," took liberties with the three unities that the older dramatists never took. A notable example is the flight from Greece, in her "dragon-car," of Medea, the barbarian princess, in his play of that name.

I do not suppose that any novelist, in any age, has ever felt himself as literally bound to observe the three unities of time, place, and action as were the ancient Greeks. Nevertheless, every novelist deals with them in one way or another. In Henry James' work, for instance, we can observe an interesting and perhaps unconscious adaptation of the unity of action. In James' later novels, as in the earlier Greek tragedies, all violence takes place off the stage. It was his theory that any "specification" was too "weak" where the strongest human emotions were involved; the reader was conducted only to the verge of an abyss and made to look over and see for himself what goes on in the depths of the human heart.

The first unity that has to be taken into consideration is the unity of place. In the next chapter I should like to consider the ways in which certain novelists observe this unity, perhaps unconsciously, when they set their stage.

Chapter Four

The Scene of a Novel

I have a friend (he is now an eminent critic) who used to say that he would write fiction if he could only figure out some way of getting people in and out of rooms. His conclusion, that since he could not do this he could not write fiction, always struck me as sound, for everything that happens in fiction must be represented as happening *somewhere,* either in some building, or in the open air, or, if you will, upon the high seas. And the house has to be built before you can induce people to walk in and out of it, just as the desert or the waste of waters must be stretched out before the moon can glint on the sand or the waves, or the trees which give a landscape its character must give the illusion of having attained a certain height before a pair of lovers can stroll beneath their boughs.

Another friend of mine—a slightly embittered editor—used to put the matter another way. He had made his own adaptation of the three unities and held that there are four questions which are answered in the first few pages of every good piece of fiction. They are: What happened? To whom did this happen? When did it happen? Where did it happen?

He himself, he said, had a simple preliminary test

for the worth of any manuscript. He did not care, he said, how attractive the hero and heroine were, how brilliant their dialogue, how exciting their adventures; if the first few pages did not reveal *where* the events related took place he did not feel that it was worth his while to read further.

When he first told me this I argued with him, to the effect that such judgment was not only harsh but unfair, but that was in the days when I myself was an aspiring author. Time and the reading of many manuscripts have led me to believe that there is some truth in what he said. His four questions, it now seems to me, are the ones that every reader would ask of every author in every age and in every country; and the author—if he is a real master—seems to answer the questions as spontaneously as the readers ask them.

The question "What happened?" cannot, of course, be answered in its entirety in the first few pages of any book, for the answer to that question is the whole action of the narrative. But you will find, I think, that in the works of any master the action "engages," as we say, immediately. Things begin happening right away. Similarly, the answer to the question "To whom did this happen?" is progressive; the whole book may be, in essence, a revelation of a person's character.

But the character of the hero or heroine of a novel reveals itself through action—through the author's portrayal of what he or she did or what happened to him or her as the result of somebody else's actions. Since a novel is concerned with what happens in this life, not the next, our hero or heroine is bound to be in one place or another throughout the whole action.

Contemporary science-fiction writers have made some interesting experiments in their attempts to prove that this is not true; they often portray characters whose adventures take place in outer space. But as far as I can see these experiments fall into two classes; either they follow the example of Swift, Wells, C. S. Lewis, or other fantasists who create imaginary worlds based on analogies to or contradictions of the world we know, or they call into play the mathematical principle of "extrapolation." In that case the reader is given a few familiar sensory data and is then, as it were, pushed into outer space, maneuvered, that is, into the position of the mathematician who if you give him part of a curve can complete its graph.

These experiments, however, are not new. A mathematician who lived long before the days of science fiction anticipated them and stated his conclusions—paradoxically: in *Alice's Adventures in Wonderland* Lewis Carroll shows the Cheshire cat's smile lingering after the cat has vanished from sight. One cannot contemplate this technical feat without a slight shiver, almost the same kind of shiver with which one would greet a ghost; the author seems to have come so near to accomplishing the impossible: the suspension of natural law. But reflection reminds us that it is a world on the other side of reality that the cat has vanished into. It is the common practice of the great masters of fiction to locate their characters firmly in both time and space before showing us what happened to them.

We do not have to look far for an august example. The first chapter of the Book of Genesis reads: "In the beginning the Lord created heaven and earth."

The words carry their own sanction. The human author cannot speak with such authority, but he must, nevertheless, imitate the Almighty as best he can. If he is going to write a novel he is faced with the task of creating an ideal world and he must create the world before he peoples it, even as the Lord created the Garden of Eden before he created Adam and Eve. This contrivance of the illusion of a universe is no light task. The Lord Himself rested on the seventh day, we are told. It is no wonder that the amateur writer shirks the attempt. My editor-friend, indeed, maintains that the ability to answer this question—we might almost say the habit of answering it—distinguishes the professional writer from the amateur. In his opinion, once a writer learns to set his stage before he endeavors to people it, he has lost his amateur standing.

Be that as it may, it is rewarding to observe how some of the masters go about preparing the stage on which the action of their narrative will take place. Professional writers sometimes call this the "Composition of the Scene"—but diffidently, almost shamefacedly. Doctors and plumbers and nuclear physicists and even painters do not hesitate to use technical terms in any conversation, and the person with whom they are talking, if he doesn't already know the term they have used, will go home and look it up in the dictionary or the encyclopedia. But let a professional fiction writer use a word that implies there is any technique involved in the writing of fiction and he will shortly be taken to task by somebody like the highly gifted John O'Hara—who maintains that Ernest Hemingway is as good a writer as Shakespeare. But I placed my back against the wall when I undertook to write this book on how to read a novel, and therefore shall employ technical terms whenever it seems necessary—as unabashedly as possible.

Let us, then, continue our examination of the practice of the masters. In Balzac, for instance, the Composition of the Scene is often given almost as much attention as the action itself. Balzac sets his stage long before he allows any one of his characters to set foot on it. Observe the first pages of *Père Goriot*:

> Mme. Vauquer, (née de Conflans) is an elderly person who for the past forty years has kept a lodging-house in the Rue Sainte-Geneviève, in the district that lies between the Latin Quarter and the Faubourg Saint-Marcel. . . . The lodging-house is Mme. Vauquer's own property. It is still standing at the lower end of the Rue Neuve-Sainte-Geneviève, just where the road slopes so sharply down to the Rue l'Arbalète, that wheeled traffic seldom passes that way because it is so stony and steep. . . . The front of the lodging-house is at right angles to the road, and looks out upon a little garden, so that you see the side of the house in section, as it were, from the Rue Neuve-Sainte-Geneviève. . . . The house itself

is three stories high, without counting the attics under the roof. It is built of rough stone, and covered with the yellowish stucco that gives a mean appearance to almost every house in Paris. There are five windows in each story in the front of the house; all the blinds visible through the small square panes are drawn up awry, so that the lines are all at cross purposes. At the side of the house there are but two windows on each floor, and the lowest of all are adorned with a heavy iron grating. . . .

The house might have been built on purpose for its present uses. Access is given by a French window to the first room on the ground floor, a sitting room which looks out upon the street through the two barred windows already mentioned. Another door opens out of it into the dining room, which is separated from the kitchen by the well of the staircase, the steps being constructed partly of wood, partly of tiles, which are colored and beeswaxed. Nothing can be more depressing than the sight of that sitting room. The furniture is covered with horsehair woven in alternate dull and glossy stripes. There is a round table in the middle, with a purplish-red marble top, on which there stands by way of ornament the inevitable white china tea service, covered with a half-effaced gilt network. The floor is sufficiently uneven, the wainscot rises to elbow height, and the rest of the wall space is decorated with a varnished paper, on which the principal scenes from *Télémaque* are depicted, the various classical personages being colored. The subject between the two windows is the banquet given by Calypso . . . displayed thereon for the admiration of the boarders, and has furnished jokes these forty years to the young men who show themselves superior to their position by

> making fun of the dinners to which poverty condemns them. The hearth is always so clean and neat that it is evident that a fire is kindled there only on great occasions; the stone chimney-piece is adorned by a couple of vases filled with faded artificial flowers imprisoned under glass shades, on either side of a bluish marble clock in the very worst taste.
>
> The first room exhales an odor for which there is no name in the language, and which should be called the *odeur de pension*. . . .

Balzac was a great writer, one of the greatest who ever lived, but this meticulous piling up of detail is clumsy. It is as if the writer were heaping up a great avalanche which is finally set in ponderous motion by its own weight. Writers who came after Balzac—some of them not half as good—have found ways of setting their stage, of composing their scene, so that things move faster and in a more lifelike way.

One of the most fascinating things about studying the works of the masters of the craft is the way in which a writer will take a device which has been used by other writers and extend it or transmute it to suit his own purposes. Gustave Flaubert rebelled against Balzac, but he learned a great deal from him in that "shock of recognition" of which I spoke earlier. One of the things he learned was the importance of the setting of the stage in any work of fiction, but his temperament did not allow him to proceed as slowly, indeed as ponderously, as the man whom he had so reluctantly taken for his master. He proceeds at a much faster pace. In *Madame Bovary* the setting plays a great part in every scene, but it is so involved with the action that it takes a cunning eye to see where setting leaves off and action begins.

The story starts with Charles Bovary's entrance into the schoolroom: "a new fellow not wearing the school uniform, and a school servant carrying a large desk. Those who had been asleep woke up, and every one rose as if just surprised at his work." [1]

> The "new fellow," standing in the corner behind the door, so that he could hardly be seen, was a country lad of about fifteen, and taller than any of us. His hair was cut square on his forehead like a village chorister's; he looked reliable but very ill at ease. Although he was not broad-shouldered, his short school jacket of green cloth with black buttons must have been tight about the arm-holes, and showed at the opening of the cuffs red wrists accustomed to being bare. His legs, in blue stockings, looked out from beneath yellow trousers, drawn tightly by braces. He wore stout, ill-cleaned, hob-nailed boots.
>
> We began repeating the lesson. He listened with all his ears, as attentive as if at a sermon, not daring even to cross his legs or lean on his elbow. . . . "Rise," repeated the master, "and tell me your name."
>
> The new boy articulated in a stammering voice an unintelligible name.
>
> "Again!"
>
> The same sputtering of syllables was heard drowned by the tittering of the class.
>
> "Louder!" cried the master; "louder!"
>
> The "new fellow" then took a supreme resolution,

> opened an inordinately large mouth, and shouted at the top of his voice as if calling someone the word "Charbovari."

It is Emma Bovary's story that Flaubert is telling, but her drama is enacted against the background of provincial life and might not have taken place if she had lived her life in a different kind of environment or had been married to another kind of man, as Baudelaire pointed out in the only commentary on *Bovary* which met with the author's approval. The pettiness, the dullness, the coarseness of life are reflected in the reactions recorded by the first narrator —a sort of "collective we"—who might stand for the picture of all rustic schoolboys. But Charles Bovary cannot cut a good figure even before these oafs, cannot even pronounce his name properly. He never "knows what it is all about."

Flaubert mingles background and action throughout *Bovary*. In his account of the first ball Emma Bovary attends at the château of the Marquis and Marchioness of Vaubyessard, the background—the hangings, the portraits on the walls, the table setting—are almost as important as what goes on in Emma's mind:

> At seven dinner was served. The men, who were in the majority, sat down at the first table in the vestibule; the ladies at the second in the dining-room with the Marquis and Marchioness.
>
> Emma, on entering, felt herself wrapped round by the warm air; a blending of the perfume of flowers and of the fine linen, of the fumes of the viands, and the odour

of the truffles. The silver dish-covers reflected the lighted wax candles in the candelabra, the cut crystal covered with light steam reflected from one to the other pale rays; bouquets were placed in a row the whole length of the table; and in the large-bordered plates each napkin, arranged after the fashion of a bishop's mitre, held between its two gaping folds a small oval-shaped roll. The red claws of lobsters hung over the dishes; rich fruit in open baskets was piled up on moss; there were quails in their plumage; smoke was rising; and in silk stockings, knee-breeches, white cravat, and frilled shirt, the stewards, grave as a judge, offering ready-carved dishes between the shoulders of the guests, with a touch of the spoon gave you the piece chosen. On the large stove of porcelain inlaid with copper baguettes the statue of a woman, draped to the chin, gazed motionless on the room full of life. . . .

But at the upper end of the table, alone amongst all these women, bent over his full plate, and his napkin tied round his neck like a child, an old man sat eating, letting drops of gravy fall from his mouth. His eyes were blood-shot, and he wore a little queue tied with a black ribbon. He was the Marquis' father-in-law, the old Duke de Laverdière, once on a time the favourite of the Count d'Artois, in the days of the Vaudreuil hunting parties at the Marquis de Conflans', and had been, it was said, the lover of Queen Marie Antoinette. . . .

The old Duke de Laverdière is an object of romantic interest to Emma—he has slept in the bed of queens—and her eyes keep turning to him throughout dinner. At the same time she shivers, and it is not only the iced champagne which the steward has just poured into her glass that makes her shiver, but the premonition of her own fate.

If one follows faithfully enough in the footsteps of the masters, one experiences delights that do not befall the impatient reader. One of these delights is the sight of one master borrowing an effect from another master and yet not losing a whit of his own originality. We observe this phenomenon often in painting; Goya's genius, for instance, is no less pronounced for his apparent debt to Gainsborough.

The careful reader will enjoy comparing the scene I have just quoted from *Bovary* with a supper that Joyce describes in a story in *Dubliners*. The tables would appear to have been set by the same hand, a hand that at a casual glance appears too lavish, indeed prodigal. We are tempted to ask ourselves why in heaven's name do they have to have so much to eat. Sober, patient reading reveals the answer: the dramatic economy of both stories requires that the boards should groan under the weight of the viands.

In *Bovary* the laden table, signifying the lavishness of the life lived by the Vaubyessards, throws into sharp contrast the life which Emma is condemned to live with her husband and which she is already beginning to find meager. The supper table set by Gabriel Conroy's aunts in Joyce's story "The Dead" serves a different function. In this story the action soars to enormous heights; the hero has a vision of all the living and the dead in the universe before he is through. Any vision or fantasy must have a solid substratum of fact if the reader is to give it what Coleridge called "the willing suspension of disbelief"—a principle familiar to all writers of science fiction. The groaning board is very important as furnishing the groundwork for belief in the architecture of Joyce's story. I suspect that if we took away one stalk of celery or one bottle of stout the whole wonderful edifice might sway and even totter.

But there is an experience even more interesting than watching one master borrow from another. It is watching a master take a method that has been used over and over again and, by extending it or exploring it more thoroughly than anybody else has ever explored it, achieve an effect which seems never to have been achieved before. In Dostoevski's *The Idiot,* the whole architectural structure is determined by the author's masterly composition of two scenes.

The Idiot begins with two young men sitting opposite each other in a railway carriage. They are talking about a young woman who is known to one of them and not known to the other.[2]

> At nine o'clock in the morning toward the end of November, the Warsaw train was approaching Petersburg at full speed. It was thawing, and so damp and foggy that it was difficult to distinguish anything ten paces from the line to right or left of the carriage windows. Some of the passengers were returning from abroad, but the third-class compartments were most crowded, chiefly with people of humble rank, who had come a shorter

distance on business. All of course were tired and shivering, their eyes were heavy after the night's journey, and all their faces were pale and yellow to match the fog.

In one of the third-class carriages, two passengers had, from early dawn, been sitting facing one another by the window. Both were young men, not very well dressed, and travelling with little luggage; both were of rather striking appearance, and both showed a desire to enter into conversation. If they had both known what was remarkable in one another at that moment they would have been surprised at the chance which had so strangely brought them opposite one another in a third-class carriage of the Warsaw train. . . .

The two young men are Prince Myshkin and Rogozhin, foils to each other throughout the action. The last scene takes place in Rogozhin's study:

There was some change in the room since Myshkin had been in it last. A heavy green silk curtain that could be drawn at either end hung right across the room, dividing the alcove where Rogozhin's bed stood from the rest of the apartment. The heavy curtain was closely drawn at both ends. It was very dark in the room. The white nights of the Petersburg summer were beginning to get darker and had it not been for the full moon, it would have been difficult to make out anything in Rogozhin's dark room with the windows curtained. It is true they could still see each other's faces, though very indistinctly. Rogozhin's face was pale as usual; his glittering eyes watched Myshkin intently with a fixed stare.

"You'd better light a candle," said Myshkin.

"No, no need," answered Rogozhin, and taking Myshkin's hand he made him sit down on a chair: he sat opposite, moving his chair up so that he almost touched Myshkin with his knees.

And so the two young men, one the embodiment of good, the other of evil, sit down, in chairs facing each other, in a darkened room, their only companion the corpse of the young woman they were talking about when we first encountered them. The stage which the author sets at the beginning of his story serves the action throughout, like the pillars of a great cathedral which, rising from the earth, soar steadily upward to form the vaulted dome. Dostoevski's adaptation of the principle of the unity of place gives his story a structure, an architecture, he could not have achieved in any other way.

The location of his story in time and space is the first problem that confronts a novelist, and the way in which he solves the problem has a great deal to do with the success or failure of his novel. But he is no sooner over that hurdle than he confronts an even steeper one: the unity of action. An important aspect—perhaps *the* most important aspect—of this problem is the attitude which the novelist takes toward his material, or, as we sometimes call it, his point of view.

Chapter Five

The Center of Vision

Percy Lubbock, in his incomparable *The Craft of Fiction,*[1] has given us what is perhaps still the most authoritative discussion of this problem of the point of view, or, as he calls it, the center of vision. Mr. Lubbock says that the art of fiction does not begin until the novelist thinks of his story as a matter to be "shown," to be exhibited so that it will seem to be telling itself. Handing over to the reader the facts of the story merely as so much information is no more, he maintains, than stating the "argument" of the book or giving the reader the groundwork upon which the novelist will build.

> The book [he says] is not a row of facts, it is a single image; the facts have no validity in themselves, they are nothing until they have been used. It is not the simple art of narrative, but the comprehensive art of fiction that I am considering. . . .

Mr. Lubbock adds that in fiction there can be no appeal to any authority outside the book itself. He maintains that the only "law" that "binds the author throughout" is

> the need to be consistent on *some* plan, to follow the principle he has adopted. . . . A critic, then, looks for the principle on which a novelist's methods are mingled

and varied—looks for it, as usual, in the novelist's subject, and marks its application as the subject is developed. But the most obvious point of method is no doubt the difficult question of the "center of vision."

The viewpoint, or the center of vision, or, as we sometimes call it, the "problem of authority," is indeed the most difficult question that confronts a writer of fiction. An author tells us that certain events took place. How do we know that he is telling the truth or that he knows what he is talking about? And did he see these events himself or is he taking somebody else's word for what happened? Onlookers, as we all know, do not always see things the same way. Anybody who has ever been involved in an accident, and consequently has had to try to report to legal authorities exactly what he saw, knows that.

The author of a piece of fiction is in somewhat the same situation as the onlooker who is being questioned by the police about the accident at the crossroads. He must report everything he saw as clearly, as precisely, as possible, but from what viewpoint? Where was he standing when the incident took place? And was the place in which he was standing one from which he could see clearly, or did some person or object obstruct his vision? The onlooker is bound by fact and cannot choose the point from which he will view the events about which he is being questioned, but the author of a piece of fiction has to choose where he will stand when viewing the events which he is asking us to believe took place, and it is up to him to choose the viewpoint most advantageous for his purposes—just as a news photographer sent out to cover a parade, say, will choose the angle from which he will take his shots.

There is, in all of us, an inherent timidity when confronted with this question. We do not want to take the responsibility. We want to invoke another authority. The ancients, who did not believe that any man "wanted to write"—as we say nowadays—but who wrote only in consequence of being possessed by a spirit other than their own, got around the difficulty by invoking their respective Muses.

Homer begins the *Iliad* by saying, "Sing, goddess, the wrath of Peleus' son. . . ."

Hesiod says, "Muses of Pieria, who glorify with song, come sing of Zeus, your father. . . ."

The writer who does not, like Homer or Hesiod, invoke supernatural authority, is hard put to make the reader even stop and listen to his story—much less believe in it. The plight of the author is boldly and beautifully dramatized in the opening stanzas of Coleridge's "The Rime of the Ancient Mariner":

> It is an ancient mariner,
> And he stoppeth one of three.
> "By thy long grey beard and glittering eye,
> Now wherefore stopp'st thou me?"

The prospective listener has every reason not to stop:

> "The Bridegroom's doors are opened wide,
> And I am next of kin;

> The guests are met, the feast is set;
> May'st hear the merry din."

But the ancient mariner

> . . . holds him with his skinny hand.
> "There was a ship," quoth he. . . .

The best man is still reluctant to listen:

> "Hold off, unhand me, grey-beard loon!"

The ancient mariner unhands him but that is only because he has got him to the point where he holds him with his glittering eye.

> The Wedding Guest stood still,
> And listened like a three years' child

as do all of us whenever we hear the opening verses of this seemingly miraculous poem.

Not all writers deal with the question as dramatically as Coleridge, but all good writers deal with it one way or another. Some writers discharge it by referring the reader from the start to another authority. They say, in effect, "Here is a story somebody told me." This is one of the most ancient devices. Chaucer used it in *The Canterbury Tales,* Boccaccio in his *Decameron,* and so did the anonymous authors of the *Arabian Nights.* Joel Chandler Harris made good use of it in his Uncle Remus stories.

One of the chief distinctions of the contemporary author William Faulkner is that in *As I Lay Dying* he has taken this ancient device and extended it, thereby achieving a dramatic effect that has not been achieved by any other living writer. The form of *As I Lay Dying* is an original contribution to the technique of the novel. The story is told by first-person narrators, but progresses, nevertheless, as swiftly and dramatically as if told by a third-person narrator. Each character seems to be intent only on revealing himself, on making you share his hopes and griefs and fears, but if you observe him closely you will see that these very confidences, which seem designed only to ease the heart of the confider, are all the while serving a dramatic purpose. There is not one of them that does not push the action forward. The form of this brilliant work might be compared to a football game in which each player, even while he dazzles the spectator with the brilliance of his play, is nevertheless carrying the ball forward a certain number of yards.

That news photographer of whom I spoke a few pages back, if he is a good photographer, will take a number of shots when he is sent out by his newspaper to cover some event, and he will take several different kinds of pictures. Some of them will be close-ups—that is, he will get as close to the object he is photographing as possible. But such photographs are often misleading. An ant-hill can look like a mountain if photographed close up. If the photographer is to make us see what the object really looks like, he will also photograph it from a distance, preferably in relation to some other object which will give us some notion of its proper dimensions.

The fiction writer has somewhat the same problem as the photographer; he can view the incidents at close quarters or from a distance. The two writers in whose hands the English novel first came to its full stature confronted this problem and made such different choices that to this day every English novelist may be thought of as following in the footsteps either of Samuel Richardson or of Henry Fielding. It is an important and fateful choice—as if a great river forked almost at its source and the traveler were obliged at the beginning of his journey to take one fork or another.

Samuel Richardson, a "master printer," who was born in 1689 and died in 1761, is generally thought of as the father of the English novel.

Professor George Sampson, in his *Cambridge History of English Literature,* says:

> The literary history of Richardson is simple. It begins with his first novel, written when he was fifty, and composed almost by accident. He had been asked by two friends, printers like himself, to prepare for them "a little volume of letters, in a common style, on such subjects as might be of use to those country readers who were unable to indite for themselves." The book came out in 1741, and is best described by its own lengthy title: "Letters written to and for particular friends, on the most important occasions. Directing not only the requisite Style and Forms to be observed in writing Famil-

iar Letters; but how to think and act justly and prudently, in the common Concern of Human Life." One of the subjects treated in this collection is the special danger attending an attractive servant girl employed in domestic service.

Out of this grew *Pamela; or Virtue Rewarded.*

Richardson discovered that if a letter is to be written it must be written by someone and addressed to someone. He does not make much of the person to whom his letters are addressed, but the adventures of Pamela, the letter writer, "in kitchen and boudoir," plunged England and all the continent into "the pleasing excitement of tears," as Professor Sampson puts it. There was also the fillip of novelty. Until that time it had never occurred to anybody that a servant girl possessed virtue to be defended.

"One would think that she was a person of quality!" a highborn lady exclaimed when Pamela, fleeing from her would-be ravisher and future husband, jumps out of a window and breaks her leg. The idea took firm hold on the popular imagination. Indeed, Queen Victoria may be thought of as the spiritual descendant of Pamela and, in a sense, as the creation of Richardson. Certainly she was the arbiter of manners and morals until recent times, when her authority was rudely challenged by another fiction writer. For the popular reader one of the charms of Ernest Hemingway's *The Sun Also Rises* is that it upholds a code of manners—and morals—which in the late twenties was coming into vogue. The first-person narrator is outspoken in his condemnation of one of the leading characters, Robert Cohn. Cohn and the heroine, Lady Brett Ashley, have spent a week end together as lovers, and now that they have returned to Paris, Cohn is not able to behave toward Brett as if they had never had this intimate relationship. The other young people are unanimous in their condemnation of Cohn's breach of the new "good manners." They all feel that he is behaving badly, when, as Brett says sadly, "he had a chance to behave so well!"

But it is Richardson's technique rather than his influence on manners and morals that concerns us here. *Clarissa* is a greater novel than *Pamela.* In his analysis of *Clarissa* in *The Craft of Fiction* Percy Lubbock says:

> [Richardson] adopts a certain artifice which carries him past the particular problem, though at the same time it involves him in several more. Little as Richardson may suspect it, he—and whoever else has the idea of making a story out of a series of letters, or a running diary written from day to day—is engaged in the attempt to show a mind in action, to give a dramatic display of the commotion within a breast. He desires to get into the closest touch with Clarissa's life, and to set the reader in the midst of it; and this is a possible expedient, though it certainly has its drawbacks.
>
> He wishes to avoid throwing Clarissa's agitations into the past and treating them as a historical matter. If they were to become the subject of a record, compiled by her biographer, something would be lost; there would be no longer the same sense of meeting Clarissa afresh, every morning, and of witnessing the new development of her wrongs and woes, already a little more poignant than

they were last night. Even if he set Clarissa to write the story in after days, preserving her life for the purpose, she could not quite give us this recurring suspense and shock of sympathy: the lesson of her fortitude would be weakened. Reading her letters, you hear the cry that was wrung from her at the moment; you look forward with her in dismay to the ominous morrow; the spectacle of her bearing under such terrible trials is immediate and urgent. You accompany her step by step, the end still in the future, knowing no more than she how the next corner is to be turned. This is truly to share her life, to lead it by her side, to profit by her example; at any rate her example is eloquently present. Richardson, or another, whoever first thought of making her tell her story while she is still in the thick of it, invented a fashion of dramatizing her sensibility that is found to be serviceable occasionally even now. . . . Her emotion . . . is caught in passing. . . . The struggles of her heart are not made the material of a chronicle. She reports them, indeed, but at such brief and punctual intervals that her report is like a wheel of life, it reveals her heart in its very pulsation. . . . The subject of her story is not in the distressing events, but in her emotion and her comportment under the strain. . . . That was what Richardson had to show, and the action of the tale is shaped round this question. . .

Richardson makes the most of it. But Lubbock continues:

He has strained this method to its utmost before he has done with it. . . . Richardson is forced to pay heavily for

> its single benefit. He pays with the desperate shifts to which he is driven in order to maintain any kind of verisimilitude. The visible effort of keeping all Clarissa's friends at a distance all the time, so that she may be enabled to communicate only by letter, seems always on the point of bearing him down. . . .

His books are, however, significant because they constitute an important stage in what Mr. Lubbock calls "the struggle to develop independent life and action." By placing himself at the very center of vision—that is, within the consciousness of his heroine—Richardson not only achieves the immediacy which is the goal of every serious novelist, but, like all the great innovators, paves the way for the triumphs of writers who come after him. In *Clarissa* he lays the groundwork for the triumphs of Henry James and the "stream of consciousness" which stood James Joyce in such good stead in *Ulysses*.[2]

Fielding's methods are very different from those of Richardson. Some learned and acute critics have argued that the "reflective" chapters with which he interspersed the narrative of *Tom Jones* actually constitute another "plane of action"—that, I believe, is E. M. Forster's phrase. Although it is possible that Mr. Forster's own infirm technique may color his critical opinions, he is not alone in this view of Fielding's method. Robert Penn Warren, who is a more accomplished technician than Mr. Forster and a more responsible critic, ranged himself on the side of the Fieldingites, I suppose, when he coined the phrase "the novel as discourse." My novelist friend X, of whom I spoke in another chapter, would consider that phrase a contradiction in terms; a novel, he would maintain, cannot consist of discourse but must consist, as he used to put it, "of action, action, and still more action." But then X is a Richardson man.

I suspect that the individual writer follows in the footsteps of Richardson or Fielding according to the dictates of his own temperament, but every fiction writer is confronted with the same choice that confronted the two early novelists: he must decide whether he will view events at close quarters or from a distance. If he chooses to view them from a distance we say that he is using the "viewpoint of the omniscient narrator."

This viewpoint—this method—would seem, at first glance, to have every advantage. The omniscient narrator not only sees everything that is going on but he also knows everything that has happened before and there is nowhere he cannot go. But prolonged consideration reveals the fact that this method—like every method—has disadvantages. The omniscient narrator is a little like a benevolent uncle who, lounging at a window, sees a procession going past down in the street and calls to his nephew to come and look, too. Uncle knows and sees everything that is going on in the street, but his window, alas, is on the second story, and even though he hoists Nephew up on the sill beside him and points out this and that object to him, Nephew, nevertheless, is inclined to feel that he would understand better what is going on if he could get down there and look for himself.

That is, he is inclined to feel that way if Uncle maintains his post at the second-story window. Since Uncle can go anywhere he wants to at any time, it is possible for him to point out alternately the whole parade to Nephew or to whisk him down to where he can see everything and everybody close up. But that requires an extraordinary amount of agility on the part of Uncle, and omniscience somehow does not encourage agility. There have been very few writers who excelled in both the "scenic" and the "panoramic" effects. Foremost among them is Leo Tolstoi, who shifts from the "scene" to the "panorama" without any apparent difficulty. Here is a passage from *War and Peace:*[3]

> Anna Pávlovna's drawing-room was gradually filling. The highest Petersburg society was assembled there; people differing widely in age and character but alike in the social circle to which they belonged. Prince Vasili's daughter, the beautiful Hélène, came to take her father to the ambassador's entertainment; she wore a ball dress and her badge as a maid of honor. The youthful little Princess Bolkónskaya, known as *la femme la plus seduisante de Pétersbourg* (the most fascinating woman in Petersburg), was also there. She had been married during the previous winter, and being pregnant did not go to any large gatherings, but only to small receptions. Prince Vasili's son, Hippolyte, had come with Mortemart, whom he introduced. The Abbé Morio and many others had also come.
>
> To each new arrival Anna Pávlovna said, "You have not yet seen my aunt," or "You do not know my aunt?" and very gravely conducted him or her to a little old

> lady, wearing large bows of ribbon in her cap, who had come sailing in from another room as soon as the guests began to arrive; and slowly turning her eyes from the visitor to her aunt, Anna Pávlovna mentioned each one's name and then left them. . . .
>
> . . . The young Princess Bolkónskaya had brought some work in a gold-embroidered velvet bag. Her pretty little upper lip, on which a delicate dark down was just perceptible, was too short for her teeth, but it lifted all the more sweetly, and was especially charming when she occasionally drew it down to meet the lower lip. As is always the case with a thoroughly attractive woman, her defect—the shortness of her upper lip and her half-open mouth—seemed to be her own special and peculiar form of beauty. Everyone brightened at the sight of this pretty young woman, so soon to become a mother, so full of life and health, and carrying her burden so lightly. Old men and dull dispirited young ones who looked at her, after being in her company and talking to her a little while, felt as if they too were becoming, like her, full of life and health.

The little Princess Bolkónskaya seems at first to have been introduced only as part of the background—*la femme la plus seduisante de Pétersbourg*—and her short, downy upper lip which does not quite cover her teeth mentioned only as one of the details which enhances her charm, until later in the evening when her husband, Prince André, takes her aside and informs her that she is to remain in the country with his father, the eccentric old Prince, while he himself is away on the campaign. Tolstoi then uses this detail which has been introduced so casually to announce a train of action: the little princess knows intuitively that this stay in the country with the half-mad old prince bodes no good for her—indeed she dies of it—and the charming little upper lip, drawn down in a grimace of pain, no longer gives her a joyful expression but makes her look rather like an animal—a squirrel or a vixen—caught in a trap.

This scene, rendered in such detail, is preceded by a panorama in which Tolstoi states his larger theme—the Napoleonic conquests and their effect upon the inhabitants of Petersburg. The setting is the drawing room of Anna Pávlovna—maid of honor and favorite of the Empress Marya Fedorovna—who is suffering from "la grippe . . . a new word in St. Petersburg, used only by the elite." Anna Pávlovna has that morning sent out, by a scarlet-liveried footman, invitations written in French, which run as follows:

> If you have nothing better to do, Count (or Prince), and if the prospect of spending an evening with a poor invalid is not too terrible, I shall be very charmed to see you tonight between 7 and 10.

The first guest to arrive is Prince Vasili Kurágin, "a man of high rank and importance." He enters wearing an "embroidered court uniform, knee breeches and shoes . . . stars on his breast and a serene expression on his flat face." Not at all disconcerted to find the "poor invalid" preparing to receive all Petersburg society, he exclaims, "Heavens, what a virulent attack!" and, at Anna Pávlovna's request, seats himself beside her on a sofa and listens patronizingly while Anna Pávlovna says—what any other noble lady, moving in court circles, might have said in July 1805:

> "Well, Prince, so Genoa and Lucca are now just family estates of the Buonapartes. But I warn you, if you don't tell me that this means war, if you still try to defend the infamies and horrors perpetrated by that Anti-Christ—I really believe he is Anti-Christ—I will have nothing more to do with you and you are no longer my friend, no longer my 'faithful slave,' as you call yourself!"

Neither the character of Prince Vasili nor that of Anna Pávlovna will receive the searching analysis which Tolstoi accords Prince André or Pierre or even Natasha. They are but mouthpieces and fade into the background once they have spoken their respective pieces. But Tolstoi manages to give even his panoramic scenes—that is, the scenes viewed, as if at a distance, by an omniscient narrator—the glitter of immediacy. This is achieved by an almost miraculously rapid alternation of viewpoint. At one moment we are called upon to survey all Europe, the next we are looking at Prince Vasili's "bald, scented and shining head" as he bows over Anna Pávlovna's hand. Very few writers have Tolstoi's agility. Once they undertake to present a panorama, they are likely to hover high over the scene, instead of darting with lightning-like speed into the thick of the action and then back to their Olympian heights.

It is interesting to compare a passage from William Makepeace Thackeray's *Vanity Fair* with these passages from *War and Peace*. Tolstoi shows us the aristocracy of Petersburg shortly before the Battle of Borodino. Thackeray shows us high society in Brussels on the eve of the Battle of Waterloo:

> There never was, since the days of Darius, such a brilliant train of camp followers as hung around the Duke of Wellington's army in the Low Countries, in 1815; and led it dancing and feasting, as it were, up to the very brink of battle. A certain ball which a noble Duchess gave at Brussels on the 15th of June in the above-named year is historical. All Brussels had been in a state of excitement about it, and I have heard from ladies who were in that town at the period, that the talk and interest of persons of their own sex regarding the ball was much greater even than in respect of the enemy in their front. The struggles, intrigues, and prayers to get tickets were such as only English ladies will employ in order to gain admission to the society of the great of their own nation. . . .
>
> On the appointed night, George, having commanded new dresses and ornaments of all sorts for Amelia, drove to the famous ball, where his wife did not know a single soul. After looking about for Lady Bareacres, who cut him, thinking the card was quite enough—and after placing Amelia on a bench, he left her to her cogitations

there, thinking, on his own part, that he had behaved very handsomely in getting her new clothes and bringing her to the ball, where she was free to amuse herself as she liked. Her thoughts were not of the pleasantest, and nobody but honest Dobbin came to disturb them.

Whilst her appearance was an utter failure (as her husband felt with a sort of rage), Mrs. Rawdon Crawley's *début* was, on the contrary, very brilliant. She arrived very late. Her face was radiant; her dress perfection. In the midst of the great persons assembled, and the eye-glasses directed to her, Rebecca seemed to be as cool and collected as when she used to marshal Miss Pinkerton's little girls to church. Numbers of the men she knew already, and the dandies thronged around her. As for the ladies, it was whispered among them that Rawdon had run away with her out of a convent, and that she was a relation of the Montmorency family. She spoke French so perfectly that there might be some truth in this report, and it was agreed that her manners were fine, and her air *distinguée*. Fifty would-be partners thronged round her at once, and pressed to have the honour to dance with her. But she said she was engaged, and only going to dance very little; and made her way at once to the place where Emmy sat quite unnoticed, and dismally unhappy. And so, to finish the poor child at once, Mrs. Rawdon ran and greeted affectionately her dearest Amelia, and began forthwith to patronize her. She found fault with her friend's dress, and her hair-dresser, and wondered how she could be so *chaussée,* and vowed that she must send her *corsetière* the next morning. She vowed that it was a delightful ball: that there was everybody that every one knew, and only a *very* few nobodies in the whole room. It is a fact, that in a fortnight, and after three dinners in general society, this young woman had got up the genteel jargon so well, that a native could not speak it better; and it was only from her French being so good that you could know she was not a born woman of fashion.

Thackeray's novels afford examples of the advantages and disadvantages of the method of the omniscient narrator. His genius was for the panorama and in *Vanity Fair* he achieves a range, a sweep of action, that he probably could not have achieved in any other way. But his scenes lack immediacy. He is weak in what Henry James called "specification." In spite of the fact that George commands "new dresses and ornaments of all sorts for Amelia," her appearance is "an utter failure." It might be better if we knew which one of her new dresses she was wearing on that particular night. We are somehow better able to appraise the character of Tolstoi's old courtier after we learn that he perfumes his bald head. But Thackeray rarely gets close enough to his scene to give the detail which could be reported only by somebody who was close at hand. He is long-winded, too, and full of stale phrases—George leaves Amelia "to her cogitations"—and worst of all, he himself often steps between us and the characters he is calling our attention to: "I have heard from ladies who were in that town at the period. . . ."

Thackeray was frankly envious of Dickens, whose genius was so unlike his own. He speaks of Dickens' apparently inexhaustible powers of invention, but it may be that what he was actually envying Dickens was his genius for the "scene." Dickens lacked Thackeray's range; his view of human nature seems crabbed and sometimes petulant as compared to Thackeray's broad compassion; in his novels the line of action is never taut, but consists, rather, of a series of brilliant episodes strung on a loose thread of narration. But nobody excelled him in the creation of a scene. Here is an example taken almost at random from *Bleak House:*

> Soon after seven o'clock we went down to dinner; carefully, by Mrs. Jellyby's advice, for the stair-carpets, besides being very deficient in stair-wires, were so torn as to be absolute traps. We had a fine codfish, a piece of roast beef, a dish of cutlets, and a pudding; an excellent dinner, if it had had any cooking to speak of, but it was almost raw. The young woman with the flannel bandage waited, and dropped everything on the table wherever it happened to go, and never moved it again until she put it on the stairs. The person I had seen in pattens (whom I suppose to have been the cook) frequently came and skirmished with her at the door, and there appeared to be ill-will between them.
>
> All through dinner; which was long, in consequence of such accidents as the dish of potatoes being mis-laid in the coal-scuttle, and the handle of the cork-screw coming off, and striking the young woman in the chin; Mrs. Jellyby preserved the sweetness of her disposition. She told us a great deal that was interesting about Borrioboola-Gha and the natives; and received so many letters

that Richard, who sat by her, saw four envelopes floating in the gravy boat.

Thackeray would never have noticed the gravy boat, much less the envelopes floating in it.

In England the Victorian author, for the most part, used a combination viewpoint of the omniscient narrator and the scenic or third-person narrator, varying the range of his camera according to whether his talent was for the panorama or for the scene. His contemporaries in France used much the same methods. Stendhal's *The Red and the Black* and *The Charterhouse of Parma* are examples of what can be accomplished by such methods in the hands of a master. Stendhal's almost Olympian attitude toward human nature lends itself particularly well to panoramic effects.

But both in England and on the continent literary craftsmen were already experimenting in the attempt to achieve a greater immediacy—to make their scenes more lifelike, more vivid. One of the boldest and most successful of these experimenters was, however, an American, Stephen Crane, who, almost singlehanded, revolutionized the short story.

Crane tells us somewhere that he got the idea for his famous *Red Badge of Courage* from one of the battle scenes in *The Charterhouse of Parma.* He does not tell us which passage furnished the inspiration, but let us compare individual scenes from the two works.[4] Fabrizio, Stendhal's hero, trying to join Napoleon's forces, wanders over the battlefield and comes upon a party of generals and their escorts. He thinks that one is the famous Marshal Ney and in his desire to get a sight of this hero follows them across the field and into battle.

> The din at that moment became terrific. . . . We must admit that our hero was very little of a hero at that moment. However, fear came to him only as a secondary consideration; he was principally shocked by the noise, which hurt his ears. The escort broke into a gallop; they crossed . . . tilled land which lay beyond the canal. And this field was strewn with dead.
>
> "Red-coats! red-coats!" the hussars of the escort exclaimed joyfully, and at first Fabrizio did not understand; then he noticed that as a matter of fact all these bodies wore uniforms. One detail made him shudder with horror; he observed that many of these unfortunate red-coats were still alive; they were calling out, evidently asking for help, and no one stopped to give it to them. Our hero, being most humane, took every possible care that his horse should not tread upon any of the red-coats. The escort halted; Fabrizio, who was not paying sufficient attention to his military duty, galloped on, his eyes fixed on a wounded wretch in front of him.

Crane, in *The Red Badge of Courage,* gets much closer to his scene:

> The youth tried to observe everything. He did not use care to avoid trees and branches, and his forgotten feet were constantly knocking against stones or getting en-

tangled in briars. He was aware that these battalions with their commotions were woven red and startling into the gentle fabric of softened greens and browns. It looked to be a wrong place for a battlefield.

The skirmishers in advance fascinated him. Their shots into thickets and at distant and prominent trees spoke to him of tragedies—hidden, mysterious, solemn.

Once the line encountered the body of a dead soldier. He lay upon his back staring at the sky. He was dressed in an awkward suit of yellowish brown. The youth could see that the soles of his shoes had been worn to the thinness of writing paper, and from a great rent in one the dead foot projected piteously. And it was as if fate had betrayed the soldier. In death he exposed to his enemies the poverty which in life he had perhaps concealed from his friends.

The ranks opened covertly to avoid the corpse. The invulnerable dead man forced a way for himself. The youth looked keenly at the ashen face. The wind raised the tawny beard. It moved as if a hand were stroking it.

"The center of vision," "the problem of authority": it is a problem which has concerned serious craftsmen of fiction since the days of Homer. Indeed, in the *Iliad,* Homer gives us one of the most skillful of all handlings of this problem, when Priam summons Helen to where the elders are sitting on the battlements of Troy and asks her to look down and identify the leaders of the Greeks drawn up below.

No writer, it seems to me, has ever introduced his

leading characters more dramatically. The drama inherent in the situation is heightened when the Greek leaders are pointed out to the Trojans by the woman they are all risking their lives for. Agamemnon appears broader-shouldered, more warlike, when viewed through the eyes of the woman who has forsaken his brother's bed and board. Indeed, he towers so high that for Helen the present moment seems unreal and she says:[5]

> That man is Atreus' son, Agamemnon, widely powerful,
> at the same time a good king, and a strong spear fighter,
> once my kinsman, slut that I am. Did this ever happen?

It is one of the most dramatic moments in all literature, so skillfully composed, so brilliantly rendered that it is no wonder that what was said on those battlements has gone echoing down through the ages. But every writer of fiction is confronted at the beginning of his book with the same problem that Homer faced in this scene: through whose eyes can he best show us what he wants us to see? Shall he, so to speak, take his stand on an eminence from which he can see everything that goes on and report what he sees from this viewpoint of the omniscient narrator? Or shall he, rather, choose one character and count on him to lead the reader into the thick of the action? If he does that we say that he is using the "scenic" method, or the method of the third-person narrator. Each of these methods, as I have tried to show, has its advantages and its disadvantages. The omniscient narrator sees everything that goes on but he does not always get close enough to the event to make the reader see it as clearly as he does. The third-person narrator has the advantage of being closer to what is going on but his viewpoint is limited; he can show us only a part of the action.

There are other methods. Two of them, the "first-person narrator" and the "effaced narrator," I will discuss in the chapter that follows.

Chapter Six

The Effaced Narrator

The best way to approach a novel is, as I have said, to follow as faithfully as possible in the footsteps of its creator. If we are to read a novel with understanding we must first of all lay aside our own preconceived idea of what a particular novel ought to be like and try, instead, to find out what it *is.* This is all the more difficult in that the author of a novel seldom—I could almost say never—knows what he is writing at the time he is writing it.

Joseph Conrad once said that writing a novel was like drifting on a rickety raft down a broad stream whose banks are so wreathed in mist that you can hardly distinguish the trees which line them, toward a waterfall whose roar is so ominous that you know your frail craft is likely to be dashed to pieces on its rocks.

The voyager, in such a situation, is inclined to be on the lookout for any safe harbor. And the broad stream—this Amazon of our imagination—has many outlets, smaller streams which will carry one eventually to the sea, but by a circuitous route. Certain technical devices, or methods, which are good enough in themselves, may be, like these smaller streams, safe for voyaging if one keeps in mind the fact that one's goal is the sea, but dangerous in that they may lead to backwaters in which a craft may be marooned.

The device of telling one's story in the first person may prove to be such a backwater if the voyager—the novelist—is not very much on his guard. There are excellent reasons for choosing to paddle up this particular stream. Some of them are so compelling that it is no wonder some voyagers mistake it for the main river. Since Stephen Crane's time, all serious writers have concentrated on the effort of rendering individual scenes more vividly; telling one's story in the first person is the easiest way to do this and the first way that comes to mind. But the method has serious disadvantages and, as a result, is suitable for only certain kinds of stories.

Its chief merit, of course, is the fact that it secures immediacy, vividness, almost automatically. Who should know better the way things happened than the person to whom they happened? And this person speaks to us in a way that commands respect and belief; that is, he seems to be speaking from the depths of his being and our attention is at once arrested. One reason the Ancient Mariner was able to make the Wedding Guest stop and listen was that the Mariner felt the tale he was telling was so important. We feel that this first-person narrator is telling the truth and a truth that is vitally important, to him at least. But he is, after all, telling us about something that happened in the past. We cannot see for ourselves what went on, we have to listen to what *he* says. As a result, he seems always to stand between us and the event unless his narration is so dramatic that we are carried away and fancy that we were present ourselves when these things happened. But inducing such self-forgetfulness demands narrative gifts of the highest order and very few writers are capable of it.

A friend of mine, the kind of person who read omnivorously all her life and with growing discernment, tells me that when she was a child she automatically rejected all novels told in the first person; she felt that "things didn't really happen" when "I" told the story. Here we have an example of a gifted child's instinctive perception of what is probably the chief disadvantage of the viewpoint of the first-person narrator.

The method has another serious disadvantage. The first-person narrator may be telling the truth, but he can only tell it as he sees it or can tell only the part of the truth that he sees. And no matter how honest he is or how keenly he feels, he may not understand what is going on.

The late Joyce Cary, in *Herself Surprised,* has used the viewpoint of the first-person narrator in a masterly way. He has turned this disadvantage, the fact that the narrator may not understand what is going on, into the very mainspring of the action. The manner of telling gives the story a superficial resemblance to *Moll Flanders,* but Mr. Cary extended Defoe's method and thereby achieved effects that Defoe never envisioned. His heroine is apparently another Moll, giving us an account of how, after a long sequence of discreditable adventures, she landed in the toils of the law. The action gains an extra fillip from the fact that she herself does not understand what she is all along revealing. She presents her adventures as discreditable to herself, and with such seeming honesty that we too are deceived and realize only at the end what the author has all along been telling us, that she is, in effect, a kind of saint, a woman who, no matter how often she is betrayed, still goes about her business of helping others.

Ernest Hemingway's novels are perhaps as good an example as one can find of the triumphs an author may achieve and the risks he inevitably runs when he uses the first person as narrator. Neither Richardson nor his great successor, James Joyce, succeeded in getting closer to his action than Hemingway does. Sound plays almost as large a part as sight in his scenes; the cadence of his sentences is such that the reader almost feels as if his own heart were beating in unison with that of the hero:

> In the late summer of that year we lived in a house in a village that looked across the river and the plain to the mountains. In the bed of the river there were pebbles and boulders, dry and white in the sun, and the water was clear and swiftly moving and blue in the channels. Troops went by the house and down the road and the dust they raised powdered the leaves of the trees. The trunks of the trees too were dusty and the leaves fell early that year and we saw the troops marching along the road and the dust rising and leaves, stirred by the breeze, falling and the soldiers marching and afterward the road bare and white except for the leaves. . . .

The action is all foreshadowed in this first paragraph of *A Farewell to Arms.* "The leaves fell early that year"—that is to say, "My love died young." It is a tale of lovers separated by early death. The very cadence of the sentences tells us what the action will gradually reveal, that, in the end, the hero's heart will be left as barren as the road along which the soldiers are marching.

The author's way of telling his story seems ideally suited to the story he has to tell. But cold reflection makes one wonder whether this method is not, after all, best adapted to certain subjects, for instance, to young love, part of whose charm is its innocence, rather than to the joys and sorrows of middle age or old age. Lieutenant Henry speaks from the heart, and the reader feels his loss so keenly that tears are likely to come into his eyes every time he reads this masterpiece.

One of Hemingway's later novels, *Across the River and into the Trees,* is told by a third-person narrator, Colonel Cantwell, but the narrator identifies himself so closely with the hero that the effect is substantially that of the first-person narrator. The middle-aged colonel is also telling the story of a lost love, but one does not feel as sympathetic with the middle-aged colonel as with the young lieutenant; it seems that at his age he ought to have known better.

But perhaps the most serious limitation of this method is that it affords little room for expansion; the action—except in the hands of brilliant inventors like Mr. Cary—is confined to the limits of the narrator's perception. This means that—in the hands of twentieth-century writers, at least—a whole dimension, the supernatural, is left out. One finds an interesting example of this limitation in a little-known playlet of Hemingway's called "Today Is

Friday," in which the author attempts to treat overtly of the relation of man to God. Three Roman soldiers are talking in a tavern after the Crucifixion:[1]

> *1st Soldier*—You see his girl?
> *2nd Soldier*—Wasn't I standing right by her?
> *1st Soldier*—She's a nice looker.
> *2nd Soldier*—I knew her before he did. [*He winks at the wine-seller.*]
> *1st Soldier*—I used to see her around the town.
> *2nd Soldier*—She used to have a lot of stuff. He never brought *her* no luck.
> *1st Soldier*—Oh, he ain't lucky. But he looked pretty good to me in there today.
> *2nd Soldier*—What became of his gang?
> *1st Soldier*—Oh, they faded out. Just the women stuck by him.
> *2nd Soldier*—They were a pretty yellow crowd. When they seen him go up they didn't want any of it.
> *1st Soldier*—The women stuck all right.
> *2nd Soldier*—Sure, they stuck all right.
> *1st Soldier*—You see me slip that old spear into him?
> *2nd Soldier*—You'll get into trouble doing that some day.
> *1st Soldier*—It was the least I could do for him. I tell you he looked pretty good to me in there today.

The beautifully rendered, expertly timed dialogue proceeds by means of bashful understatements. Christ, suffering on the Cross for the sins of mankind, does not elicit any more eloquence from the writer than a courageous but unlucky prize fighter could have called forth. At the end of the dialogue the Second Soldier makes a comment familiar to Hemingway's readers: "You been out here too long. That's all." Man, remaining just as he is, undergoing, that is to say, no spiritual change, may yet solve his problems by going on—or going back—to a country where everything will be "fine." Hemingway's early heroes are rarely middle-aged persons. They are returned soldiers, or adolescents, or Spaniards like the bull-fighter Manuel Garcia, or expatriates like Jake Barnes, seeking the answer to the question they are forever asking by returning to lost innocence or taking up their abode in some foreign land.

A similar accusation cannot be brought against Hemingway's gifted contemporary William Faulkner. Mr. Faulkner seems to have an instinctive perception of the pitfalls lying in wait for the first-person narrator. His stage is large enough to include human beings of every kind. The range of his creation includes not only normal people but characters whose consciousness is below the human level: Benjy in *The Sound and the Fury* and the idiot in *The Hamlet,* who crowns the object of his affections, a cow, with a chaplet of flowers that might have come out of a Greek pastoral. But his characters, if they sometimes descend below the threshold of human consciousness, also venture beyond it. His archvillain, Flem Snopes, goes to hell and engages in a contest with the Devil. Eula, Flem Snopes' wife, is a goddess-like creature who, in answer to the cries of men who come up the moonlit road seeking her father, stands suddenly at a window looking down on them, as Helen of Troy looked down on the Achaians from the battlements of Troy:

> She did not lean out, she merely stood there, full in the moon, apparently blank-eyed or certainly not looking downward at them—the heavy gold hair, the mask not tragic and perhaps not even doomed: just damned, the strong faint lift of breasts beneath the marblelike fall of the garment; to those below what Brunhilde, what Rhinemaiden on what spurious river-rock of papier-mache, what Helen returned to what topless and shoddy Argos, waiting for no one. . . .

Mr. Faulkner, for all his lapses into bathos,[2] will loom large, I think, when the history of the novel is written. Certainly he is one of the boldest and most successful experimenters the craft has known. Both *The Sound and the Fury* and *As I Lay Dying* are significant contributions to form. *The Sound and the Fury* is, truly, a "tale told by an idiot." Using an "innocent eye" as his center of vision Faulkner achieves dramatic effects comparable to those achieved by Henry James in his "later method." In *As I Lay Dying* Faulkner has taken one of the oldest fictional devices—a collection of tales told by pilgrims to entertain or enlighten fellow pilgrims—and has evolved a unique vehicle for narrative, has broken a record, for this particular story proceeds at a faster pace than any other contemporary fiction.

Even when he is not using the first-person narrator, or an adaptation of that method, Faulkner achieves a vividness, an immediacy, that is achieved by few of his fellow writers. He may never have read Henry James, but he seems to have profited considerably from the example of James' great contemporary, Gustave Flaubert. All of Faulkner's work is characterized by what (keeping a wary eye on O'Hara) I shall venture to call "Flaubertian three-dimensionalism."

Flaubert never told you what a flower, for instance, was like. Instead, he tried to give you the illusion, by the use of sensory details, that you could not only look at the flower he was presenting for your admiration but could smell it and feel the texture of its petals. In *A Simple Heart* he writes:

> On days when it was too hot they did not leave their room. From the dazzling brilliance outside light fell in streaks between the laths of the blinds. There were no sounds in the village; and on the pavement below not a soul. This silence round them deepened the quietness of things. In the distance, where men were caulking, there was a tap of hammers as they plugged the hulls, and a sluggish breeze wafted up the smell of tar.

In "Spotted Horses" Faulkner writes:

> From Mrs. Littlejohn's kitchen the smell of frying ham came. A noisy cloud of sparrows swept across the lot and into the chinaberry tree beside the house, and in the high soft vague blue swallows stooped and whirled in erratic indecision, their cries like strings plucked at random.

Homer uses sensory details in much the same way. In the *Iliad,* after the priest, Chryses, has prayed to Apollo, the Greeks

> first drew back the victims' heads and slaughtered them and flayed them, and cut slices from the thighs and wrapped them in fat, making a double fold, and laid raw collops thereon, and the old man burnt them on cleft wood and made libation over them of gleaming wine; and at his side the young men held in their hands five-pronged forks. Now when the thighs were burnt and they had tasted the vitals, then sliced they all the rest and pierced it through with spits and roasted it carefully, and drew all off again. . . .

But Flaubert's handling of the center of vision, or the problem of authority, is perhaps his greatest contribution to the craft. In *Madame Bovary* he grapples with this problem and solves it in a way which had not been used before. His method becomes apparent with our first glimpse of his heroine. We see Emma first as a young woman "in a blue merino dress with three flounces" who comes to the door of the Rouault farmhouse to welcome the young doctor, Charles Bovary, who has come there to set her father's broken leg. While the doctor is setting the broken bones

> Mademoiselle Emma tried to sew some pads. As she was a long time before she found her workcase, her father grew impatient; she did not answer, but as she sewed she pricked her fingers, which she then put to her mouth to suck them. Charles was surprised at the whiteness of

> her nails. They were shiny, delicate at the tips, more polished than the ivory of Dieppe, and almond-shaped. Yet her hand was not beautiful, perhaps not white enough, and a little hard at the knuckles; besides it was too long, with no soft inflections in the outlines. Her real beauty was in her eyes. Although brown they seemed black because of the lashes, and her look came at you frankly, with a candid boldness.

It is Charles who perceives how white Emma's nails are, but it is Flaubert himself, not Charles, who perceives that while Emma's nails are "shiny, delicate at the tips, more polished than the ivory of Dieppe," that her whole hand is, nevertheless, not beautiful. It is too hard at the knuckles, with no soft inflections in the outlines. She is not the woman Charles thinks she is, or, indeed, the woman *she* thinks she is. Flaubert is using two viewpoints in this passage, that of Charles and that of the narrator, who is faced with the necessity of getting as close to the action as if he were a first-person narrator, and yet who must never appear on the scene in person.

Flaubert was well aware of the problems he faced. He wanted the first-hand impression, the vividness he would have achieved by having Emma tell her own story, but he wanted more than that. He wanted a viewpoint as immediate as that of Emma herself and at the same time more sophisticated. Emma has captivated the imagination of readers for more than a century, but we are attracted to her not by her intellect but by her complex emotional nature. Flaubert felt the necessity of bringing to bear on the happenings an intellect more acute than Emma's, of wider range. He therefore evolved the viewpoint which I have called the effaced narrator.

Throughout the action Flaubert maintains, with an almost incredible agility, the vantage point that is best suited to the moment he is rendering:

> At the bottom of her heart, however, she was waiting for something to happen. Like shipwrecked sailors, she turned despairing eyes upon the solitude of her life, seeking afar off some white sail in the mists of the horizon. She did not know what this chance would be, what wind would bring it her, towards what shore it would drive her, if it would be a shallop or a three-decker, laden with anguish or full of bliss to the portholes. But each morning, as she awoke, she hoped it would come that day; she listened to every sound, sprang up with a start, wondered that it did not come; then at sunset, always more saddened, she longed for the morrow.

That is Flaubert speaking, standing far enough away from his heroine to view her with detachment. But he will stand sometimes at Emma's elbow, as it were. When she looks into the mirror he reports not only what she sees but things that she herself could never observe:

> In spite of her vapourish airs (as the housewives of Yonville called them), Emma, all the same, never seemed gay, and usually she had at the corners of her mouth that immobile contraction that puckers the faces of old maids, and of those men whose ambition has failed. She was pale all over, white as a sheet; the skin of her nose was drawn

> at the nostrils, her eyes looked at you vaguely. After discovering three grey hairs on her temples, she talked much of her old age. . . .

But sometimes he, so to speak, slips inside his heroine, sees with her eyes, hears with her ears, as in the famous scene in the attic where Emma has fled on receiving a letter from Rodolphe breaking off their illicit affair:

> . . . she went on up the stairs, breathless, distraught, dumb, and ever holding this horrible piece of paper, that crackled between her fingers like a plate of sheet-iron. On the second floor she stopped before the attic-door, that was closed.
>
> Then she tried to calm herself; she recalled the letter; she must finish it; she did not dare to. And where? How? She would be seen! "Ah, no! here," she thought, "I shall be all right."
>
> Emma pushed open the door and went in.
>
> The slates threw straight down a heavy heat that gripped her temples, stifled her; she dragged herself to the closed garret-window. She drew back the bolt and the dazzling light burst in with a leap.
>
> Opposite, beyond the roofs, stretched the open country till it was lost to sight. Down below, underneath her, the village square was empty, the stones of the pavement glittered, the weathercocks on the houses were motionless. At the corner of the street, from a lower story, rose a kind of humming with strident modulations. It was Binet turning.
>
> She leant against the embrasure of the window and re-read the letter with angry sneers. But the more she

fixed her attention upon it, the more confused were her ideas. She saw him again, heard him, encircled him with her arms, and the throbs of her heart, that beat against her breast like blows of a sledge-hammer, grew faster and faster, with uneven intervals. She looked about her with the wish that the earth might crumble to pieces. Why not end it all? What restrained her? She was free. She advanced, looked at the paving-stones, saying to herself, "Come, come!"

The luminous ray that came straight up from below drew the weight of her body towards the abyss. It seemed to her that the ground of the oscillating square went up the walls, and that the floor dipped on end like a tossing boat. She was right at the edge, almost hanging, surrounded by vast space. The blue of the heavens suffused her, the air was whirling in her hollow head; she had but to yield, to let herself be taken; and the humming of the lathe never ceased, like an angry voice calling to her.

Here we see Flaubert's effaced narrator at work. Flaubert does not *tell* us how Emma felt when she read her lover's letter. He renders her anguish by showing us her reactions to the heat of the attic, the sight of the weathercocks on the neighboring houses, to the very cobblestones of the village square, which, as she looks down at them, seem to be rising up to meet her, and as a last touch her reaction to the savage, monotonous humming of Binet's lathe, which seems to be calling to her to throw herself out of the window.

Flaubert evolved his effaced narrator out of his necessity. He is not the first writer to have used the method, but he is the first to use it consistently for a conscious purpose, and by so doing he has put all novelists who come after him in his debt.

It seems to me that in recent times there has been a tendency to underestimate his contribution, to give up without much of a struggle the ground he fought so hard to gain. Contemporary writers are fully as much concerned with the problem of achieving immediacy as he was, but many of them try to attain it in the easiest way, that of the first-person narrator. The first-person narrator is well suited to certain kinds of stories but we have seen that except in the hands of bold and skillful experimenters like Joyce Cary the method has serious limitations. The voyager who follows the procession of boats up that particular inlet may find himself in a backwater, may have to paddle back up to the main stream if he is ever to reach the sea—that is, if he is to make his contribution to the art of fiction. The greatest technical triumphs which have been achieved so far by any novelist seem to me to be solidly based on Flaubert's achievement—seem, indeed, an extension of his effaced narrator. It is Henry James' distinction to have brought this effaced narrator out of hiding, to have made him take the center of the stage and perform in a way no narrator before him has ever performed.

Chapter Seven

Henry James and His Critics

When I think of Henry James and his critics I am reminded of the blind men who were taken to see the elephant and asked to tell what it was. One got hold of the elephant's leg and said that it was a tree; one got hold of its trunk and said that it was a snake, perhaps a boa constrictor—and so on. Many of James' early critics were blinded by their own preconceptions, which kept them from making any serious effort to find out what manner of creature they were dealing with.

H. G. Wells said about James' style, in *Boon, the Mind of the Race:*[1]

> James begins by taking it for granted that a novel is a work of art that must be judged by its oneness. Someone gave him that idea in the beginning of things and he has never found it out. He doesn't find things out. He doesn't even want to find things out. He accepts very readily and then—elaborates. . . . The only living human motives left in his novels are a certain avidity and a certain superficial curiosity. His people nose out suspicions, hint by hint, link by link. Have you ever known living human beings do that? The thing his novel is *about* is always there. It is like a church lit but with no congregation to distract you, with every light and line

> focussed on the high altar. And on the altar, very reverently placed, intensely there, is a dead kitten, an egg shell, a piece of string. . . .

Wells liked his parody so much that he sent it to Henry James, apparently thinking, E. M. Forster says in *Aspects of the Novel,* that "the master would be as much pleased by such heartiness and honesty as was Wells himself." James seems to have been more impressed by Wells' obtuseness than by his "heartiness and honesty," and a rather sharp interchange of letters followed. Mr. Forster says:

> Beyond the personal comedy, there is the great literary importance of the issue. It is this question of the rigid patterns: hour-glass or grand chain or converging lines of the Catherine Wheel, or Bed of Procrustes—whatever image you like as long as it implies unity. Can it be combined with the immense richness of material which life provides? Wells and James would agree it cannot; Wells would go on to say that life should be given the preference, and must not be whittled or distended for a pattern's sake. My own prejudices are with Wells. The James novels are a unique possession and the reader who cannot accept his premises misses some valuable and exquisite sensations. But I do not want more of his novels . . . just as I do not want the art of Akhenaton to extend into the reign of Tutankhamen.

F. R. Leavis in his comments on *The Golden Bowl,* the novel which was the crown of James' lifework, finds

James deficient in moral sense. *The Golden Bowl* is a novel whose action hinges on an illicit love affair. Charlotte Verver, who is still a young woman, is having an affair with her husband's son-in-law, Prince Amerigo, an Italian nobleman. Prince Amerigo's wife Maggie, finds out about the affair and through her patience, perspicacity, and charity wins back the love of her husband while preserving as far as is possible the happiness of her father and his errant wife. The action is complicated, indeed made possible, by the fact that Maggie Verver, who is unusually devoted to her father, has been instrumental in bringing about his marriage to a young wife; she has done this in order to be free to enjoy her own happiness with the Prince, but instead Charlotte's entrance into the circle comes near wrecking Maggie's marriage. She and her father have doubtless been guilty of the sin of using another fellow creature for their own convenience. Yet Charlotte, apparently, is not interested in any other man and accepts the middle-aged widower of her own free will. Mr. Leavis says:

> If our sympathies are anywhere, they are with Charlotte and (a little) the Prince, who represent what, against the general moral background of the book, can only strike us as a decent passion; in a stale, sickly and oppressive atmosphere they represent life.

In an encounter between Maggie and Charlotte, James represents Charlotte as evil personified, "seated at its ease." In a remarkable figure he has also portrayed her as a monster with harpy-like claws, whose bestial passions are kept in check by a silken cord about her neck, a cord whose end her husband holds in his hand. But Mr. Leavis does not seem to have taken these passages into account—passages in which the author states his own moral judgment of his character.

Rebecca West thinks that James was too fastidious to write good novels. She says:

> He never perceived that life is always a little painful at the moment, not only at this moment but at all moments; that the wine of experience always makes a raw draught when it has just been trodden out from the bruised grapes by the pitiless feet of men, that it must be subject to time before it acquires suavity.

Mr. Van Wyck Brooks goes even further in his adverse criticism of James. He says:

> The behaviour of his characters bears no just relation to the motives that are imputed to them. They are "great," they are "fine," they are "noble"—and they surrender their lovers and their convictions for a piece of property. They are "eminent" and their sole passion is acquisitiveness. Magnificent pretensions, petty performances!—the fruits of an irresponsible imagination, of a deranged sense of values, uncorrected by any clear consciousness of cause and effect.

I do not believe that any great writer has ever been more misunderstood and misrepresented—in short, so badly read. It is pleasant to reflect that the state of affairs is changing and James is coming into his own. There have been a great many books written about his work in the past fifteen years and some of them contain valuable perceptions. Perhaps the most important is Joseph Warren Beach's *The Method of Henry James.*[2] Mr. Beach's procedure is different from that of many of James' other critics. Instead of drawing his conclusions from whatever part of the elephant's body his hand happens to fall upon, he has examined the whole creature and then provoked it to trumpet before deciding what kind of creature it is. He takes a hint about the nature of James' work from one of James' own characters. In "The Figure in the Carpet" the novelist Hugh Vereker tells the narrator, who is an ardent admirer of his work, "There's an idea in my work without which I wouldn't have given a straw for the whole job . . . and the application of it has been, I think, a triumph of patience, of ingenuity. . . . It stretches, this little trick of minc, from book to book. . . . The order, the form, the texture of my books will perhaps some day constitute for the initiated a complete representation of it. . . ."

The other man says, "You call it a little trick?" and the novelist replies, "That's only my little modesty. It's really an exquisite scheme."

Mr. Beach's book is a careful and patient analysis of the "exquisite scheme" with which, he thinks, James was concerned all of his professional life, at first blunderingly, almost unconsciously, and as time went on with more and more awareness of the technical problems involved. Mr. Beach says, "His little trick was simply not to tell the 'story' at all as the story is told by the Scotts and Maupassants, but to give us instead the subjective accompaniment of his story. His 'exquisite scheme' was to confine himself as nearly as possible to the 'inward life' of his characters." To those critics who complain that nothing much happens in a James novel, Mr. Beach would reply that a great deal goes on but that it goes on at a level deeper than the level to which James' contemporaries penetrated. He says:

> The world of James is at once more strange and more familiar than that of the traffic jam or the dime store. It is a strange world indeed in which one is concerned with nothing but the essentials. It is strange, too, for people who keep constantly to the superficial levels of consciousness, when, like visitors to mines, a smoky lamp is fixed to their caps and they are taken for excursions through dark subterranean galleries. . . . In the stories of other writers men and women are shown to us obsessed with desires and ambitions and oppressed by material difficulties. And our interest is absorbed in the process by which they overcome their difficulties and realize their desires. The characters of James too have ambitions and desires. But that is not the thing that strikes us most about them. What strikes us about them is their capacity for renunciation—for giving up any particular gratification in favor of some fine ideal of conduct with which it seems incompatible. . . . The characters of James are not common men and women; and for the finest of them there is always something of more account than the substance of their experience—namely its quality. They may, like other mortals, long for the realization of some par-

> ticular desire; but they long still more fervently for the supreme comfort of being right with themselves.

They are, in short, fitted for the adventures that await them, and these adventures, even though they may begin in a London drawing room to the tinkle of teacups, will lead them into as dark and as subterranean chambers as have yet been explored by any fiction writer.

Mr. Beach, in *The Twentieth Century Novel,* portrays James as doing what no novelist before him had succeeded in doing—uniting the apparently diverse streams of the narrative and the dramatic; or perhaps it might be better to say that in his hands the narrative undergoes a transformation and becomes the dramatic. Mr. Beach calls him the "chief exemplar of the dramatic method."

> It is this type of structure that sharply distinguishes his work from that of authors like Thackeray, say, or H. G. Wells, who are always *telling* the readers what happened instead of showing them the scene, telling them what to think of the characters rather than letting the reader judge for himself, or letting the characters do the telling about one another.

In our own day Somerset Maugham is perhaps the foremost exponent of the method of "telling" as opposed to that of rendering dramatically. Most of Mr. Maugham's stories are told by the same narrator, a benevolent, sophisticated, rather languid world traveler, who somewhat resembles Mr. Maugham himself. In *Christmas Holiday* Mr. Maugham treats the same subject that Henry James treats in *The Ambassadors:* a man's whole life is changed as the result of a stay in Paris and his meeting with a certain woman. James never appears on his scene. His heroine reveals herself gradually, through events, through what her friends say about her, and through the conclusions the hero finally arrives at. Mr. Maugham's method is in sharp contrast. When it is necessary for his hero to know something about the heroine's past life, he suspends the thread of his narrative long enough to let her tell him about it—at considerable length. Her life has been eventful. Her husband is serving a term on Devil's Island and she is working in a house of prostitution because of her conviction that she can best help him expiate his crime by humiliating herself. It is contact with these people's blind, overmastering desires that, as Mr. Maugham puts it, makes the bottom drop out of the young Britisher's comfortable middle-class life. But, alas, we know these crimes and passions only at second and third hand—when the heroine tells us about them. The author in so openly consulting his own convenience has sacrificed the effect of lifelikeness. One finds oneself wondering whether any young man, on his first vacation in Paris, would have listened so patiently and so long to the story of anybody else's life, no matter how colorful.

James himself said that the novelist's foremost concern was "the vivid image and the very scene." The key to his later method lies in his idea of what constitutes a scene. Mr. Beach points out that for James the word "scenic" means "dramatic." James conceives of the novel in terms of the scene, or picture (something to be looked at, watched, not talked about) and thereby has almost brought about a "reversal of the essential method of fiction":

> The essential method of fiction is, or always has been, narrative. The earliest English novels consisted of a series of adventures, whose thread might generally be cut off anywhere with little damage to any plot there was. . . . The early conception of the novel when conscious of form was in terms of the epic narrative, as appears in the theory of Fielding and in the practice notably of Fielding and Scott. And this continues to be the conception of the English novel down to the time of Henry James. . . . But in the most distinctive work of James the sense of progress, of story, is almost altogether lost. You have rather a sense of being present at the gradual uncovering of a wall painting which had been whitewashed over and is now being restored to view. The picture was all there from the start; there is nothing new being produced. . . . The stages are merely those by which the exhibitor or restorer of the picture uncovers now one, now another, portion of the wall or canvas, until finally the whole appears. . . . Or, once more to vary the figure, it is as if a landscape were gradually coming into view by the drawing off of veil after veil of mist. You become aware first of certain mountain forms looming vaguely defined. Little by little the mountains take on more definite shape, and something can be made out of the conformation of the valleys. And very slowly, at length, comes out clear one detail after another, until in the end you command the whole prospect, in all its related forms and hues.

Chapter Eight

The Central Intelligence

Percy Lubbock, in *The Craft of Fiction,* calls the method which Henry James finally evolved the "viewpoint of the central intelligence." James' central intelligence is not omniscient, but his very lack of knowledge is made to serve him as powerfully as knowledge would have served him. He is closer to the happenings than other narrators; the sensory impressions he records are as vivid as those of any first-person narrator, and his scenes are as "pictorial" as Dickens'. But he is not subject to the limitation of the other narrators. In one leap James seems to have hurdled all the obstacles which have confronted other fiction writers. His viewpoint of the central intelligence as it reveals itself in his last three great novels, *The Ambassadors, The Wings of the Dove,* and *The Golden Bowl,* is perhaps the greatest technical triumph which the novel has known in its short history.

In his notebooks James sometimes called the method which he spent his life discovering and perfecting "the great compositional law," but he referred to it oftenest as the "divine principle of the scenario," and he discovered it while trying to write plays. The life of a great writer is a mysterious affair. It is possible that everything that happens to him is grist for his mill. Henry James' family and friends, and many of his critics, did not seem to understand the significance of his experience in the theater. Leon Edel thinks that James' writing for the theater was a "manifestation of an inner conflict" that went on all his life. Mr. Edel says:

> For him . . . the theatre became the focus of anxiety, fear, insecurity, conflicting emotions which caused him to approach it with faltering steps. A work of fiction might receive adverse reviews and fall flat in the market and still remain an honorable experience; it did not involve the public *exposure* that went with a play. . . . A choice between Boston (home, art, the study) and Europe (the world) had imposed itself and he had made it, although in reality without resolution of the inner conflict.

I feel sure that Mr. Edel is right in one respect: there was an "inner conflict" going on in James; but I cannot believe that it was a choice between his own country and Europe. He had already solved that problem. James, early in his life, acknowledged Balzac as his master. He points out that Balzac's prodigious achievement was made possible by his whole-hearted commitment to his subject matter—and he had chosen all France as his subject. A disciple submits himself to the discipline of a master in order to learn all that the master knows. It is a commonplace among painters that a great master is often excelled by his pupil, or sometimes we see three great painters linked one after another in that "shock of recognition" of which I spoke earlier: Gian Bellini, Giorgione, and Titian are examples.

But since fiction differs from other art forms in being concerned with the conduct of life itself, as Jacques Maritain has pointed out, these discernments are not made as easily as in the considerations of other art forms. As far as I know, F. W. Dupee and the late Edna Kenton are the only literary critics who have expressed the opinion that James, in choosing to live abroad rather than in America, was not "fleeing" America but was rather making the same passionate commitment to his own country that his master, Balzac, had made to France.

The pupil, however, excelled the master in this case. Balzac dealt with only one country. James is a colossus who bestrides two continents. The action of his novels takes place in Venice, Florence, Rome, or London, but his subject is the impact of America on Europe. Nothing happens until the Americans come on the scene. This is apparent in one of his early works, *The American.* Claire de Cintré and her brother Valentin were languishing in well-bred desiccation until Christopher Newman came into their midst. Prince Amerigo in *The Golden Bowl* is like a great golden statue fixed in a niche until his American bride and her father set him in motion.

Worldly considerations, too, may have impelled James toward the theater. He was fifty-two years of age. He had published his first story when he was twenty-two. During all the years he had been writing fiction he had had only one popular success, with *Daisy Miller,* and that success lay twenty years behind him. As he approached his later method his books grew more and more unpopular, especially when serialized in magazines. One editor complained that he "killed the subscribers off like flies." It may have been partly as the result of his finding more difficulty in magazine publication that James turned to writing plays, and for five years maintained, with what seems a singular lack of perspicacity, that in the play he had found his "real form."

This illusion was rudely shattered when *Guy Domville* was produced in London. A few critics praised it half-heartedly but the public rejected it whole-heartedly. James was hissed when, as the result of a blunder on the part of the management, he took a curtain call. William James gave an explanation for the fiasco which to this day is accepted in many quarters. Henry, William said, had "drifted so far from the vital facts of human character that he could hardly hope to express human tensions." Henry James' experiences in the theater seemed, indeed, a disaster when viewed from the worldly standpoint. One would have thought that the five years he put in trying to learn how to write plays were wasted, but the passage of the years puts matters in a different light. Those years now reveal themselves as the most rewarding and fructifying of James' professional career, for it was during those apparently wasted years that he laid hold of the great technical secret which makes his later work different from his earlier work and, indeed, different from that of any novelist who had gone before him.

James himself did not seem to realize this for some months. But then the meaning of his failure as a playwright burst upon him and he wrote of the public's rejection of his play:[1]

> If there has lurked in the central core of it this exquisite truth . . . that what I call the divine principle of the scenario is a key that, working in the same general way, fits the complicated chambers of *both* the dramatic and the narrative lock: if, as I say, I have crept round through long apparent barrenness, through suffering and sadness intolerable to that rare perception—why my infinite little loss is converted into an almost infinite little gain.

And at the beginning of the new year he, as it were, re-dedicated himself to his art: "I take up my own old pen again—the pen of all my old unforgettable and sacred struggles. To myself—today—I need say no more. Large and full and high the future still opens. It is now indeed that I may do the best work of my life. And I will."

What is this "divine principle of the scenario" which James wrested from his bitter failure on the stage and applied to the technique of the novel? It is, to begin with, I think, a closer approximation of reality, of lifelikeness, than any other novelist writing in English has yet attained, and it was achieved by a union of the narrative and dramatic techniques. The key to his method lies in the way in which he presents his characters for our consideration—in much the same way life presents characters for our consideration. His people reveal themselves to us gradually—the way people reveal themselves to us in life.

James has practically obliterated himself as narrator. His stories are not told; they are acted out as if on a stage.

He does not *tell* you anything about his characters; he lets them reveal themselves to you by what they say and do. He has added to this another device which works powerfully for verisimilitude. His characters not only reveal themselves to us by what they themselves say and do but are further revealed by being shown to us through the eyes of their families, their friends, their enemies, and their acquaintances. Until we stop to think about it, it is hard to realize what a large part such a process plays in our own lives. Our opinions, our estimations of people's characters, are based, to a great extent, on their relationships to other people. It is as if we arrived at our relationships with a person only through his relationships with others.

Joseph Warren Beach has pointed out that James' first use of his later method was in *The Portrait of a Lady*. It is significant that the preface to *The Portrait* should contain James' own statement of his "great compositional law," which is, so he says, to employ but one "centre of vision," that of the hero or heroine, and to refer everything that happens to this consciousness. In his preface to *The Portrait* he presents his great technical discovery in the form of a metaphor, one of those figures of speech with which he sometimes clarifies a train of thought much as a lightning flash may illuminate a whole countryside:[2]

> The house of fiction has in short not one window, but a million,—a number of possible windows not to be reckoned, rather; every one of which has been pierced, or is still pierceable, in its vast front, by the need of the individual vision and by the pressure of the individual will. These apertures, of dissimilar shape and size, hang

so, all together, over the human scene that we might have expected of them a greater sameness of report than we find. They are but windows at the best, mere holes in a dead wall, disconnected, perched aloft; they are not hinged doors opening straight upon life. But they have this mark of their own that at each of them stands a figure with a pair of eyes, or at least with a field glass, which forms again and again, for observation, a unique instrument, insuring to the person making use of it an impression distinct from every other. He and his neighbors are watching the same show, but one seeing more where the other sees less, one seeing black where the other sees white, one seeing big where the other sees small, one seeing coarse where the other sees fine . . . there is fortunately no saying on what, for the particular pair of eyes, the window may *not* open. . . . The spreading field, the human scene, is "the choice of subject"; the pierced aperture, either broad or balconied or slit-like and low-browed, is the "literary form": but they are, singly or together, as nothing without the posted presence of the watcher—without, in other words, the consciousness of the artist.

The windows are of all sizes and shapes but they all have a common outlook: onto the broad meadow that surrounds the mansion. We may think of this broad meadow as representing the human scene, the raw material out of which a novelist makes his fiction. In James' figure each window represents the work of one fiction writer. The window may be as broad, say, as the outlook which the

Greek tragedian Aeschylus had on humanity, or as narrow as the least skillfully executed modern detective story, but each writer looks out on the same broad meadow—that is to say, every piece of fiction that was ever written has the same subject: what happened to certain human beings. The individual book will vary according to the size of the window; the book a man writes represents his outlook on life.

Some of what James says is not new to us. We have heard it before from various writers, or have come to the same conclusions from our own experience. But when he tells us that at each of these windows a figure stands, holding a pair of field glasses, he tells us something that nobody else has told us. This is the heart of his great technical discovery. At first glance it seems absurd. It is only when we ponder on the implications of what he says that its full meaning reveals itself to us. The existence of a window implies the existence of a room. The figure of which he speaks stands at the window. The first thing that occurs to us when we are considering the condition of a human being is whether he is alone or companioned by someone else. James' figure at the window is not alone. The next thing we have to determine is the identity of his companion.

His companion is, I think, the reader of a piece of fiction. His situation is different from that of the figure of whom we are speaking. He does not stand at the window as the figure does. Indeed, he does not seem to have access to the window. We may almost think of him as a willing prisoner—imprisoned, that is, within the cell of his own consciousness. There is a paradox here; the prisoner's only access to the "outside" world—that is, the world "inside" the novelist's consciousness—is through the figure at the window. James, in his later method, establishes a bond between the reader and the author closer than that established by any other novelist. This relationship is set forth—paradoxically—in his brilliant metaphor of the "figure at the window."

A novel—any piece of fiction—is a kind of closed circle. It exists, first of all, within the imagination of the writer, and the reader cannot step into this closed circle unless the writer invites him to do so. The imagination of the writer is the stage on which his characters act out their parts. The only way the reader can know what goes on on that stage is from what the writer tells him or shows him. All techniques of fiction, therefore, reduce themselves, in the end, to one problem: how can the writer best persuade the reader to step inside the charmed circle of his imagination and how can he induce him to linger there long enough to observe what goes on on that stage?

As for the reader, if he accepts the author's invitation he must, it seems to me, lay aside his own opinions and predilections and, as Coleridge put it, "listen like a three years' child"—till the time comes for him to step out of the charmed circle and back into his own world. But the first step for the reader, in James' method, is the fixing of his attention on the "figure at the window."

James' figure at the window communicates his knowledge to the reader in a way unlike any of those which his predecessors have used. He does not call to the reader to come and let him hoist him up on the window ledge where he can see everything that goes on; he does not point out occurrences of particular interest down below, or, turning his back on his post, recount the tale of his own trials and triumphs. Instead, he keeps his post at the window and asks only one thing of the reader: that he will look steadily and attentively into his eyes. If the reader has a keen pair of eyes himself and is capable of sustained effort he will see more by this method than is revealed by a casual glance. But, at any rate, that is all that is required of him by this method: to look into another man's eyes and see what is mirrored there.

It would seem that the reader's vision will be greatly circumscribed if he sees only what is mirrored in one pair of eyes. But that, after all, is all that one sees ordinarily—the human scene viewed through one pair of eyes, our own. A novel which uses the combination of the omniscient and scenic viewpoints gives you only one man's vision of events, that of the author, while the first-person narrator gives you an even more restricted vision, that of the hero-narrator. James' method actually doubles the vision; we have two pairs of eyes viewing events instead of one.

This sounds very simple, on the surface, but it is actually difficult to grasp and difficult to apply to the understanding of fiction. Percy Lubbock puts it well when he says that the "real actors in *The Ambassadors* are the thoughts, emotions and sensations of the hero"—Lambert Strether. Strether is never off the stage and everything that happens is, in the end, referred to him and evaluated by him. It would seem that this method would considerably restrict the author. If everything has to be rendered through the eyes of the "central intelligence," will not certain scenes have to be foregone, since he cannot be everywhere and see everything? Actually this is not the case. James gets some of his most dramatic effects from the fact that Strether has not been everywhere and, in his fifty-four years, has seen comparatively little. James himself says, "Strether's sense of these things, and Strether's only, should avail me for showing them; I should know them but through his more or less groping knowledge of them, since his very gropings would figure among his most interesting motions. . . ."

The viewpoint of the central intelligence is a sort of Archimedean lever by which a fiction writer not only calls his imaginary world into being but also keeps it in motion—if he retains firm enough grasp on his lever.

James has said that his discovery is a key that, working in the same general way, fits the complicated chambers of *both* the "dramatic and the narrative lock." This remark attracted little attention when it was made—naturally enough, since it appears in his communings with his Muse in his notebooks. But it marks an important milestone in the history of the novel. It is as if the author has for a long time been toiling up a slope steep enough to be almost insurmountable and, suddenly emerging onto the top of the mountain, stops long enough to look back on the way he has come. One of the sights which James could and did view metaphorically from his mountaintop was the merging of the two mighty streams of English fiction into one swift-moving current. In his later method he has accomplished the seemingly impossible, reconciling techniques that until his day seemed diametrically opposed to each other; he is as immediate, as dramatic, as Richardson in his crucial scenes, but the chapters which lead up to those scenes, in much the same way that the broad slopes lead up to the mountaintop, exhibit narrative gifts as impressive as those of Fielding.

In the development of the novel as an art form there has been an ever-increasing emphasis on the dramatic. Readers may ask, why, if this is so, does the novelist keep on writing novels; why does he not write plays instead? The answer to this question is, I think, that part of the uniqueness of the novel as an art form is that it can borrow from other forms and at the same time remain true to the laws of its own being. A novelist's best scenes are certainly those which are most dramatic, those which are most like the scenes enacted on a stage. But in achieving such effects a novelist has infinitely more freedom of movement than a dramatist. Through a central intelligence he can make comments on other characters and reveal the meaning of actions in ways which are not available to a dramatist, whose medium is too compressed for their use. Through the central intelligence viewpoint a novelist has another supreme advantage denied to the dramatist: he can get inside the consciousness of at least one of his characters; a dramatist must render all his characters from outside.

The advantages accruing to a novelist from an emphasis on dramatic rather than narrative representation are seen most clearly, perhaps, in the later novels of Henry James. His last three great novels, *The Ambassadors, The Wings of the Dove* and *The Golden Bowl,* are all examples of this method. The serious reader is perhaps best advised, however, if he first makes the acquaintance of the method in *The Ambassadors,* which James himself spoke of as "quite the best, 'all round,' of my productions."

The Ambassadors is the dramatization of what happened to a middle-aged man, Lambert Strether, as the result of a stay of some months in Paris. He is sent there by his fiancée, a resolute, wealthy New England widow, whose only son, Chadwick Newsome, has been living for some years in Paris. Mrs. Newsome wants her son to come home and take charge of the family business. She surmises that he would have come home long since if he were not involved with some woman, and she wants Strether to rescue her son from the clutches of this woman, who, she is convinced, can be only a designing hussy. Strether is somewhat of the same opinion when he undertakes the mission. We are introduced to him at the moment he first sets foot in England, arriving at Chester. He has expected his friend, the American lawyer Waymarsh, to meet him there, but Waymarsh has not come. Instead, Strether makes the acquaintance of an American lady, Maria Gostrey, who is one of those characters whom James once spoke of as "running beside the coach."

Maria Gostrey serves to prepare us—and Strether—for the entrance upon the scene of the heroine, Madame de Vionnet, by being unlike any woman Strether has ever known before. She is, as she tells him, "a general guide to Europe." She says, "I wait for people. I put them through. I pick them up—I set them down. . . . I bear on my back the huge load of our national consciousness. . . ."

On his arrival in London Strether dines with Miss Gostrey before going to the opera. He has accompanied his wealthy, middle-aged fiancée to the opera in Boston, but on those occasions he has never dined with her at a table "on which the lighted candles have rose-coloured shades." He is struck, too, by the difference between Miss Gostrey's appearance and that of Mrs. Newsome on similar occasions. Mrs. Newsome, when she attends the opera, wears a white ruche on the high collar of her dress. Miss Gostrey's dress is "low-cut" and she wears "round her throat a broad red velvet band with an antique jewel." Strether has told Mrs. Newsome that her ruche makes her look like Queen Elizabeth. Miss Gostrey reminds him of Mary Queen of Scots. Everybody knows that it was easier for men to fall in love with Mary Queen of Scots than with Queen Elizabeth. We all know, too, that Mary Queen of Scots met a hard fate at the hands of her envious cousin. This scene beautifully foreshadows the treatment that Chadwick Newsome's friend, Madame de Vionnet, will receive at the hands of Mrs. Newsome.

E. M. Forster has compared the form of *The Ambassadors* to a kind of dance, a stately, slow minuet in which the characters, starting at opposite sides of the room, gradually change places. That is, the characters whom, in the beginning, we are inclined to think of as the "bad people" are shown, in the end, to have been all along on the side of virtue, and those who announce themselves as virtuous are revealed, finally, as not being quite as good as they would have us think they are. But the meaning of Mr. Forster's figure is not apparent till the end of the book.

Lambert Strether finds that his mission will have to remain in abeyance for some weeks; Chad Newsome is out of town and Madame de Vionnet, whose name has been associated with his, is reported to be in the south of France. Strether, meanwhile, enters the circle of Chad's acquaintance, but it is not until he has been in Paris for some weeks that he meets Madame de Vionnet.

James has given her what painters call a "long foreground"; she does not come on the scene until the eleventh chapter. James sets his stage carefully, a tea party in the garden of the famous sculptor Gloriani:

> The place itself was a great impression—a small pavilion, clear-faced and sequestered, an effect of polished *parquet,* of fine white panel and spare, sallow gilt, of decoration delicate and rare, in the heart of the Faubourg Saint Germain and on the edge of a cluster of gardens attached to old noble houses.

The party adjourns to the garden at the back of the house. Strether is talking with Chad's friend, John Little Bilham, and is asking him what Madame de Vionnet is like when Bilham sees Chad emerging from the house and says, "He has come to take you to her."

We see Madame de Vionnet through Strether's eyes:

> She was dressed in black, but in black that struck him as light and transparent; she was exceedingly fair, and, though she was as markedly slim, her face had a roundness, with eyes far apart and a little strange. Her smile was natural and dim; her hat not extravagant; he had only perhaps a sense of the clink, beneath her fine black sleeves, of more gold bracelets and bangles than he had ever seen a lady wear.

It is astonishing how much dramatic tension James has got into this scene when apparently all he is doing is calling our attention to a beautiful woman. But it is all there in this one passage, everything that Strether is to find out and to pay a fearful price for finding out—all there, if he had the wit to see it, just as, no doubt, the meaning of the life of any one of us is compressed into some single incident whose significance eludes us at the time.

Madame de Vionnet is a lady of the *haute noblesse* but she has already broken with the conventions that govern the conduct of women of her class and is living apart from her husband, the Comte de Vionnet. The fabric of her dress is not only light but transparent; her situation is known to everybody in her social circle—to everybody, that is, except Lambert Strether, who thinks that Chad Newsome is in love not with her but with her daughter.

Madame de Vionnet, though she is markedly slim and fair, has "a roundness" of the cheeks, and her eyes are "far apart and a little strange." She is a woman who may not look at life from the conventional viewpoint, may look at things in a way that would seem shocking to Woollett, Massachusetts. And then, to make sure that we get his point, James underlines it: under her thin black sleeves Madame de Vionnet wears more gold bracelets and bangles than Strether has ever seen a lady wear before. She is a lady of the *haute noblesse* and she is also a woman who is capable of having an illicit love affair.

Strether registers all these impressions when he first sees her, but it is not until later that he realizes their significance. Chad has all along wanted to take him to call upon Madame de Vionnet, but he has refused to go. He has begun to suspect, however, that the marked improvement he has observed in Chad is due to her influence and finally agrees to pay the visit. Her surroundings make an even deeper impression on him than Gloriani's garden had made:

> She occupied, his hostess, in the Rue de Bellechasse, the first floor of an old house to which our visitors had had access from an old clean court. The court was large and open, full of revelations, for our friend, of the habit of privacy, the peace of intervals, the dignity of distances and approaches; the house, to his restless sense, was in the high, homely style of an elder day, and the ancient Paris that he was always looking for—sometimes intensely felt, sometimes more acutely missed—was in the immemorial polish of the wide waxed staircase and in the fine *boiseries,* the medallions, mouldings, mirrors, great

clear spaces, of the grayish-white salon into which he had been shown.

Chad leaves the two together. Madame de Vionnet is "seated, near the fire, on a small, stuffed and fringed chair, one of the few modern articles in the room; and she leaned back in it with her hands clasped in her lap and no movement, in all her person, but the fine, prompt play of her deep young face." Strether has "an extraordinary sense of her raising from somewhere below him her beautiful suppliant eyes. He might have been perched at his door-step or at his window, and she standing in the road. . . . 'What can I do,' he finally asked, 'but listen to you as I promised Chadwick?' "

She asks him to tell Mrs. Newsome that he likes her and her daughter, and if he can't quite do that she asks, "Will you consent to go on with me a little—provisionally—as if you did?" Strether, still under the impression that Chad is in love with her daughter, promises to "save" her if he can. And now comes a kind of shifting of spiritual gravity on which the whole action turns. Strether, when he first arrived in Paris, told Chad that he thought he ought to go home. Chad temporizes and asks him "to wait a while and see," promising that he *will* go home if Strether comes to feel that that is really what he ought to do.

Strether, by this time, is well acquainted in Chad's circle of friends and discusses Chad's character with some of them. And here we see the beautiful use James makes of the "runners beside the coach," characters who are not vitally involved in the action and yet constantly promote it. Chief among these characters are Maria Gostrey and John Little Bilham. Maria Gostrey professes the utmost admiration for Madame de Vionnet, but actually leaves town in order not to be involved in a situation which she foresees is going to be a matter of life and death for her friend. When she comes back she tells Strether that she is not going to receive Madame de Vionnet if she should call upon her. This puzzles him very much. He is also puzzled by conversations he has had with Chad's friend, Little Bilham. When Strether comments on the improvement he has noticed in Chad, Bilham agrees but says he isn't sure that Chad "was meant to be that good." These "runners beside the coach," not having their attention wholly centered on the occupants of the coach, look ahead and see what is waiting at the next bend in the road long before the hero has any idea of what is going to happen. This device is of great dramatic value; it serves to prepare the reader for what is to come. If he were not given this preparation he might not accept what comes.

Strether, brooding over the complications of his new life, wanders out into the open country for a day. Toward evening he comes upon a rustic inn on the bank of a river and is arranging with the *patronne* to give him dinner in a pavilion at the garden's edge when he sees a boat advancing around a bend in the river. It is being rowed by a young man in his shirt sleeves, and a lady sits in the stern of the boat, holding a pink parasol. Strether recognizes the couple as Madame de Vionnet and Chad. They greet him with marked cordiality and insist on his dining with them there in the pavilion. Madame de Vionnet is unusually gay throughout the evening, and so talkative that when Strether gets back to his hotel he sits down on his bedroom sofa and stares straight before him for a long time. Only now does he fully realize what everybody else has known all along, that Madame de Vionnet and Chadwick Newsome have been lovers for some time.

The next morning he gets a note from Madame de Vionnet asking him to come to see her, and he goes to her apartment on the Rue de Bellechasse. Again James sets his scene very carefully and, as in the scene in which he first presents Madame de Vionnet, everything is implicit from the beginning:

> The light in her beautiful formal room was dim . . . the hot night had kept out lamps, but there was a pair of clusters of candles that glimmered over the chimney-piece like the tall tapers of an altar. The windows were all open, their redundant hangings swaying a little, and he heard once more, from the empty court, the small plash of the fountain. From beyond this, and as from a great distance—beyond the court, beyond the *corps de logis* forming the front—came, as if excited and exciting, the vague voice of Paris. Strether had all along been subject to sudden gusts of fancy in connection with such matters as these—odd starts of the historic sense, suppositions and divinations with no warrant but their intensity. Thus and so, on the eve of the great recorded

> dates, the days and nights of revolution, the sounds had come in, the omens, the beginnings broken out. They were the smell of revolution, the smell of the public temper—or perhaps simply the smell of blood.

Miss Gostrey, Madame de Vionnet's forerunner, reminded Strether when he first dined with her of Mary Queen of Scots. In this scene the figure is extended. Madame de Vionnet is dressed this evening in "simplest, coolest white, of a character so old-fashioned, if he were not mistaken, that Madame Roland, on the scaffold, must have worn something like it." It is no accident that Madame de Vionnet on this evening reminds him of Madame Roland, for this evening marks the execution of all of Madame de Vionnet's hopes.

Strether realizes that her discomposure is too deep to be caused by last night's *contretemps* alone. He reflects that to deal with women "was to walk on water."

> . . . What was at bottom the matter with her, embroider as she might and disclaim as she might—what was at bottom the matter with her was simply Chad himself. It was of Chad she was, after all, renewedly afraid; the strange strength of her passion was the very strength of her fear; she clung to him, Lambert Strether, as to a source of safety she had tested.

"You're afraid for your life!" he blurts out. She tells him that she is "old and abject and hideous. . . . There's not a grain of certainty in my future; for the only certainty is that I shall be the loser in the end"; and she wants to know if he cannot be persuaded to remain in Paris; she feels the need of seeing him and talking with him. But he has made up his mind to go.

Lambert Strether enters Chadwick Newsome's circle of acquaintance an innocent. That is one of his charms for these sophisticated worldlings, and all through the action there is a sort of conspiracy to preserve his innocence. Bilham tells him that the attachment between Chad and Madame de Vionnet is "virtuous," though he knows that he and Strether have different interpretations of the word, and Maria Gostrey goes out of town to avoid being questioned about her friend's situation. Among James' greatest technical triumphs are several scenes in which everybody in the room knows what is being talked about—except Strether. He preserves his innocence—that is to say, his gift of simplicity, which is in itself a kind of genius—but it undergoes a transformation. At the beginning of the action he not only did Mrs. Newsome's bidding but he admired her, and now Mrs. Newsome is revealed as coarse and unfeeling and Madame de Vionnet, "the designing hussy," at the end seems to Strether the noblest woman he has ever known, a woman who has opened to him a world which up to the time he met her had existed only in his imagination. But it is not only Mrs. Newsome and Madame de Vionnet who have changed sides in the dance—to use Mr. Forster's apt figure. Strether himself has changed, has developed, as a result of his adventures in Paris, into the man he was meant to be. The innocent, the American as opposed to the European, is revealed as the wisest of them all, even wiser and nobler than Madame de Vionnet.

He goes back to America to face a poor future as far as material fortunes go. He will not marry the wealthy widow, and he will no longer be editor of the literary review which was dependent on her patronage. We can be certain, however, that he will continue to grow spiritually; and we can be equally certain that Chadwick Newsome has turned his back on whatever spiritual good he may have derived from his association with Madame de Vionnet.

Percy Lubbock, in *The Craft of Fiction,* has compared James with Giotto, the first western painter to "put air around the heads of his figures." That is to say, the figures in his paintings have a kind of monumentality which the painters before him—Cimabue and Duccio, for instance—never achieved. One feels as if one could walk behind one of Giotto's figures, take the path that curves around one of his rocks or through a little wood. James' method of the central intelligence produces the same effect of solidity, of lifelikeness. One is in no doubt as to what happened to Lambert Strether—or to Madame de Vionnet or Chadwick Newsome, for that matter—but when we have put the book down our imaginations come back from time to time to dwell on them and we can fancy them going on in life, as people do go on even after the most exciting adventures.

Lubbock points out that there are "kinds of virtuosities in any art which affect the whole of its future; painting can never be the same again after some painter has used line and colour in a manner that his predecessors had not developed, music makes a new demand of all musicians when one of them has once increased its language." The analogy is rewarding. James has used the technical resources of his craft as they were used by no other novelist before him. His discovery of a key that fits both the dramatic and the narrative lock may be compared, I think, to those discoveries made by Sophocles which Aristotle sets forth and analyzes in the *Poetics*. Certainly they are as revolutionary in his time as Sophocles' discoveries were in his day, and may constitute a new point of departure for the craft. The novel, instead of being dead or moribund as an art form, may be on the threshold of its development. At any rate, all serious readers of fiction would do well to contemplate the enormous vista opened by James' discoveries about the structure, the *architecture,* of the novel.

James was concerned with style, too; one of the highest praises he could give a novel was to say that it was "written"—by which he meant that every word in the novel was chosen with the view to its playing a certain part in the structure of the whole. The French call a word so selected and placed *le mot juste,* the "right" word for which there is no substitute because it is the only word which will express what the writer wants to say. James was well aware that, on the whole, French novels are better written than English novels, word for word. His earlier novels have an almost Gallic lucidity and grace. The novels which are the crown of his life's work—*The Ambassadors,*

The Wings of the Dove, The Golden Bowl—are not, on the whole, as well written.

In the next chapter I would like to consider some of the requirements of a good prose style—and the paradoxical situation of a great writer who, at the end of his career, was not writing so well, sentence by sentence, paragraph by paragraph, as when he started.

Chapter Nine

Tone, Style, and Controlling Metaphor

John Rodker once remarked of Ford Madox Ford's *The Good Soldier* that it was the "only French novel written in English," by which I take it, and Mr. Ford himself took it, that this particular novel had a quality which has distinguished the French novel and which has been conspicuously lacking in the English novel. Various names have been given to this quality by writers who have striven to achieve this almost indefinable effect. We sometimes call it "tone," as if we were speaking of a piece of music. Certainly *The Good Soldier* is as carefully composed as a piece of music. It was called originally *The Saddest Story,* and the action is presented by a first-person narrator. It is, indeed, a sad story that he tells, but it is by no means unique. In fact, it is one of the oldest and, at the same time, commonest of dramatic situations: the triangle, the husband involved with another woman or the wife involved with another man. Mr. Ford's action involves two married couples and he throws in, for good measure, a young girl with whom the hero falls in love after he has exhausted the possibilities for misbehavior in his intimate circle. The young girl goes mad, another young woman who has been swept into the orbit of the two couples dies of heart failure as the result of emotional shock, and the two chief characters commit suicide. Mr. Ford's problem, as I see it, is not so much convincing the reader that these things happened as convincing him that the characters were so conscienceless, blind, willful, or mad as not to foresee the horrors that were sure to come.

The action of the narrative is so closely knit that it does not lend itself easily to analysis, but we believe, at least while we are reading the story, that things happened the way the narrator says they happened. The author persuades us, I think, through "tone." A man who came into a room full of merrymakers to announce that the whole city was on fire would not command attention unless he instinctively suited the tone of his voice to the extraordinary nature of his message. Every remark that Ford's narrator makes carries its own conviction; the tone is perfectly suited to the action. His way of achieving this effect is to keep reminding us of the human condition, for almost every sentence is a little world in itself, in which man's ineptitude, feebleness, blindness, are constantly measured against the infinite.

"Edward has not been dead a month and already there are rabbits on the lawn," Edward's widow Leonora says, turning away from the drawing-room window, and this posing of the finite against the infinite—the tiny creatures never dared caper on the lawn as long as Edward was alive—makes us aware, as no words of mourning could make us aware, of Edward's changed condition.

Ernest Hemingway is also a master of tonal effects.

Very often the tone of one of his paragraphs is made to serve as part of the action. In *The Sun Also Rises* the hero, Jake Barnes, is incapable of making love to any woman as the result of a wound he has sustained in the war, and the woman he is in love with has gone off with a young bullfighter. His friends, Mike and Bill, are going back to Paris in search of excitement, but he does not want to go to Paris. "It would have meant more fiesta-ing. I was through with fiestas for a while."

> I went in and ate dinner. It was a big meal for France but it seemed very carefully apportioned after Spain. I drank a bottle of wine for company. It was a Chateau Margaux. It was pleasant to be drinking slowly and to be tasting the wine and to be drinking alone. A bottle of wine was good company. Afterward I had coffee. The waiter recommended a Basque liqueur called Izzarra. He brought in the bottle and poured a liqueur-glass full. He said Izzarra was made of the flowers of the Pyrenees. It looked like hair-oil and smelled like Italian *strega*. I told him to take the flowers of the Pyrenees away and bring me a *vieux marc*. The *marc* was good. I had a second *marc* after the coffee.

There is in the very tone of this paragraph a sort of summing up of what has gone before. The tone sheds such light on the happenings that we realize, almost with a start, to what a pass the hero has been brought; he has no hopes, no aspirations, and in his despair he has rejected, at least for the moment, any companionship except the gratification of his own senses.

Such tonal effects call for the unerring selection of the right word for the right place. When a friend suggested to Flaubert that he remove a phrase from his masterly *A Simple Heart* he replied that he could not do so; if he removed a word the whole story would collapse.

James' "written" had, for him, the same connotation as the French use of *le mot juste*—a novel in which every word played its part. It is ironical, for this reader at least, that James should use such an expression. The Freudian literary critics are all insistent that Henry James sustained a "psychic wound" in his youth that lasted all his life. I feel sure that he did sustain a grievous psychic wound in early youth, but I suspect that they err in its location. His wound was in his Achilles heel and he sustained it not through "sibling rivalry" but at the hands of his father. I refer to the misfortune this great writer suffered in being exposed throughout his formative years to his father's prose style.

The elder Henry James was an amateur philosopher and theologian—a brilliant man, but so eccentric and impatient of restraint that he never subjected himself or any of his children to any prolonged intellectual discipline. The novelist Henry James has said in *Notes of a Son and Brother* that the atmosphere of the James household reflected what the children and their mother called "Papa's ideas." The child Henry James thought of "Papa's ideas" as being housed in a sort of temple which occupied the foreground of the family hearth. He thought of his mother as a priestess, sitting on the steps of the temple, tending beakers of the divine fluid that had been placed about handily for any passer-by to quaff. "I cannot remember," James adds, "that any of us ever quaffed any of the fluid."

It is apparent that none of the young Jameses ever willingly absorbed any of the "divine fluid," but there are other things going on in temples besides communions, and when incense is burned on any altar its particles rise on the air to disseminate themselves imperceptibly. The novelist Henry James, even while he rejected "Papa's ideas," was unconsciously subjected to his father's prose style and the influence of a prose style can linger, like incense on the air, long after its echoes have died away. The speech which William Faulkner, for instance, delivered on the occasion of his receiving the richly deserved Nobel Prize falls on the (Southern) ear with some of the same cadences as a speech which the Southern orator Henry W. Grady delivered in Buffalo, New York, shortly after the Civil War, and Henry W. Grady's periods, like those of every orator of his generation, were modeled on Cicero's addresses to the Roman Senate on the discovery of Catiline's conspiracy.

The elder Henry James' impatience and eccentricity are reflected in his prose style. His earlier writings were, for the most part, negative criticisms of religious orthodoxy; his later writings were concerned with the tenets of "The New Church," of which, as somebody remarked, he was the only member. Austin Warren, in his *New England Saints*,[1] points out that Mr. James always defined his own position "by its contrariety to current views in philosophy and science as well as religion," and adds that "For all his fond addiction to verbal distinctions, he uses terms freely, not consistently."

One of the elder James' books is called *Society, the Redeemed Form of Man: An Earnest of God's Providence.* The title is an earnest of his prose style. The philosopher, whose bent of mind was primarily theological in spite of his lifelong battle with orthodox religious belief, regarded the Cambridge horsecar as "Our True Schechinah at This Day" and spoke of its "frankly chaotic or a-cosmical aspect":

> I nevertheless continually witness so much mutual forbearance on the part of its *habitués;* so much spotless acquiescence under the rudest personal jostling and inconvenience; such a cheerful renunciation of one's strict right; such an amused deference, oftentimes, to one's invasive neighbor: in short, and as a general thing, such a heavenly self-shrinkage in order that "the neighbor," handsome or unhandsome, wholesome or unwholesome, may sit or stand at ease: that I not seldom find myself inwardly exclaiming with the patriarch: *How dreadful is this place! It is none other than the house of God, and the gate of heaven!*

William James, who confessed that the posthumous editing of his father's literary remains was the hardest task he ever faced, said:

> Whenever the eye falls upon one of Mr. James' pages —whether it be a letter to a newspaper or to a friend, whether it be his earliest or his latest book—we seem to find him saying again and again the same thing; tell-

> ing us what the true relation is between mankind and its Creator. What he had to say on this point was the burden of his whole life, and its only burden. When he had said it once, he was disgusted with the insufficiency of the formulation (he always hated the sight of his old books), and set himself to work to say it again. But he never analyzed his terms or his data beyond a certain point, and made very few fundamentally new discriminations; so the result of all this successive re-editing and repetition and amplification and enrichment . . . [was monotony] rather than reconstruction. The student of any one of his works knows, consequently, all that is *essential* in the rest.

A style whose chief characteristic is repetitiousness is not fitted for the fine discriminations which Henry James the elder spent his life trying to make. The novelist has given an affecting picture of his father as his family found him, seated

> each long morning, at his study table either with bent considering brow or with half-spent and checked intensity, a lapse backward in his chair and a musing lift of perhaps troubled and baffled eyes. . . . He applied himself there with a regularity and a piety as little subject to sighing abatements or betrayed fears as if he had been working under pressure for his bread and ours and the question were too urgent for his daring to doubt.

Mr. Warren continues the picture:

> There he sat at his desk, composing his papers as though the world were seriously eager for them, and

> revising and correcting as though competent judges were to pass them in review. It is incredible that he did not generally write rapidly and with fervor; but Henry recalls his now and then leaning back from his desk, "again and again, in long fits of remoter consideration, wondering, pondering sessions into which I was more often than not moved to read . . . some story of acute inward difficulty amounting for the time to discouragement."

One is tempted to wonder whether the elder Henry James might not have done better if he had addressed his considerable talents to the writing of only one book and the writing of it well. His thoughts press so hard one on the other, and he succumbs so often (within a single paragraph) to the temptation to express himself paradoxically, if not contrarily, that he seldom succeeds in writing a decent sentence.

But the sentence is the basis of a good prose style, "the unit of prose," as Sir Herbert Read has pointed out in his valuable book, *English Prose Style*.[2] He follows Jespersen in holding that primitive language was not differentiated into parts of speech but consisted rather of "long words full of difficult sounds, and sung rather than spoken." He defines a sentence as "a single cry":

> . . . its various qualifications, length, rhythm and structure . . . determined by a right sense of this unity. In a sentence the rhythm keeps close to the inner necessities of expression; it is determined in the act of creation. It is the natural modulation of the single cry.

The prose style of Henry James the novelist grew more complicated the longer he lived. Various reasons are given for this. Those who are inclined to take a superficial view of his work say that it was because he dictated his later novels. His more discerning admirers hold that the complexity of his later style is the result of the fact that as he grew in stature he had more to say and therefore needed a longer sentence to say it in. I think that there is a good deal of truth in this view. The novelist's early style is, as I have said, distinguished by lucidity and grace and he deals more than competently with his subject matter. If his literary career had ended with the publication of *Daisy Miller* or even *The Bostonians* there would have been ready for him a safe and comfortable niche in our Hall of Fame. His was the harder and more stirring fate of the author whose works are not really read in his lifetime for the reason that his readers are not yet born. (James, during his lifetime, did not have a single discerning reader, as his notebooks testify. "Oh, if there only *were* a reader!" he once exclaimed.) I suspect that when he put his early triumphs behind him and began his subterranean explorations into the abysses that underlie all human conduct he was deeply influenced by his father's example of saintliness and lifelong dedication to an ideal so high that it seemed almost impossible of realization, and, finding himself committed to the same high adventure, unconsciously echoed the cadences which recorded his father's agonized and seemingly unsuccessful search for the eternal verities. To a sensitive ear James' prose—in his later novels

—is unmodulated and lacking in one of the foremost requirements of a good style: balance.

Read says:

> The danger with all long and complex sentences is that they may lack balance. The sense may be logically clear, the rhythm may be easy, but still they try our patience and offend our sensibilities. There is a want of proportion between the subject and the predicate, or between either of these and the verb—not so much a proportion of sense, which would result in humour, but a proportion of structure, the simple against the complicated, the devious against the direct.

Yeats has spoken of what he calls the "numb line," the line in a poem which, being in itself "relaxed," serves to heighten by contrast the intensity of the line that follows it. Such an effect is rarely come upon in Henry James' sentences. The simple is seldom posed against the complicated, the devious against the direct. Complication, rather, follows complication, one indirection often seems to beget another, until we are sometimes in danger of losing the point of what James has to say through his earnest effort to keep saying more and more.

Here is an example taken at random from *The Ambassadors:*

> His impression of Miss Gostrey after her introduction to Chad was meanwhile the impression of a person almost unnaturally on her guard. He struck himself as at

first unable to extract from her what he wished; though indeed *of* what he wished at this special juncture he would doubtless have contrived to make but a crude statement. It sifted and settled nothing to put to her *tout bêtement,* as she often said, "Do you like him, eh?"—thanks to his feeling it actually the least of his needs to heap up the evidence in the young man's favour.

James, for the most part, writes only one kind of sentence. It is rather long and bristles with subordinate clauses, with qualifications; he hardly gets one thing said before he starts saying another. There is something amateurish about the general run of James' sentences. They are like a young author's first novel: it does not occur to him that he may live to write another and he puts in all the furnishings of his imagination. A first book often has enough material in it for half a dozen. So James often seems to be attacking each sentence as if it were to be the last he would ever write. Everything that comes into his mind on this particular subject at that moment is packed into one sentence, which often breaks in two under the weight imposed on it; the reader's attention is likely to stray midway of the sentence whereas he might have held on to the end if the author had demanded less of him.

Compare the passage I have just quoted with Joyce's *Dubliners* or his *Portrait of the Artist.* Joyce has at his command a variety of sentences. He uses often a short, declarative sentence, unqualified by subordinate clauses; a longer sentence which often appears in the middle of the paragraph as a sort of connective, which may or may not have subordinate clauses; and, finally, the long sonorous sentence which is the crowning glory of his prose style. Consider the last paragraph of "The Dead":[3]

> A few light taps upon the pane made him turn to the window. It had begun to snow again. He watched sleepily the flakes silver and dark, falling obliquely against the lamplight. The time had come for him to set out on his journey westward. Yes, the newspapers were right! Snow was general all over Ireland. It was falling on every part of the dark central plain, on the treeless hills, falling softly upon the Bog of Allen, and, farther westward, softly falling into the dark mutinous Shannon waves. It was falling too upon every part of the lonely churchyard on the hill where Michael Furey lay buried. It lay thickly drifted on the crooked crosses and headstones, on the spears of the little gate, on the barren thorns. His soul swooned slowly as he heard the snow faintly through the universe and faintly falling, like the descent of their last end, upon the living and the dead.

Each of Joyce's sentences is modulated. So are his paragraphs. The modulation—it is actually a rhythm—carries on from one paragraph to another. But rhythm, if it is to please the ear, must have variations—in paragraphing as well as in the individual sentence. If every paragraph on a page has the same rhythm the effect is monotonous. In Joyce a short, so to speak staccato, paragraph is often followed by a paragraph which is not only longer but has a looser rhythm.

Read has pointed out that there is in good writing "a visual actuality. It exactly reproduces what we should metaphorically call the contour of our thought." James' paragraphs *look* ugly on the page. Each paragraph, when it is not broken by conversation, is a solid block whose size and shape seem to have been determined not by any consideration of pleasing or luring the reader, but by the amount of endurance the author was able to muster. His paragraphs end only when he comes, for the moment, to the end of his endurance. The fact of the matter is that James in early youth was not subjected to any of the disciplines and was exposed to but few of the models which ordinarily play an important part in the formation of a good prose style.

There is something else which I think ought to be taken into consideration in any discussion of the work of this great writer and that is the peculiar quality of his imagination. Coleridge, in a recorded conversation, has made a distinction between two kinds of writers, which is, I think, applicable to James. Coleridge said:[4]

> There are two kinds of talkative fellows whom it would be injurious to confound, and I, S. T. Coleridge, am the latter. The first is of those who use five hundred words more than [they need] to express an idea. . . . The second sort is of those who use five hundred more ideas, images, reasons, etc., than there is any need of to arrive at their object, till the only object arrived at is that the mind's eye of the bystander is dazzled with colours succeeding so rapidly as to leave one vague impression that there has been a great blaze of colours all about something. Now

> this is my case and a grievous fault it is. My illustrations swallow up my thesis. I feel too intensely the omnipresence of all in each, platonically speaking. . . . Bring me two things that seem the very same, and then I am quick enough [not only] to show the difference, even to hair-splitting, but to go on from circle to circle till I break against the shore of my hearer's patience, or have my concentricals dashed to nothing by a snore. . . .

Read, in the introduction to his valuable book, considers whether there is an "absolute or pure prose style, to which all styles approximate, or against which all styles are to be judged" and reaches the conclusion that Dean Swift's style comes closer to approximating this perfection than that of any other English prose writer. Almost any page of *Gulliver's Travels* affords examples of the chief excellence of Swift's prose style:

> I lay down on the grass, which was very short and soft, where I slept sounder than ever I remember to have done in my life, and as I reckoned, about nine hours; for when I awaked it was just daylight. I attempted to rise, but was not able to stir: for as I happened to lie on my back, I found my arms and legs were strongly fastened on each side to the ground; and my hair, which was long and thick, tied down in the same manner. I likewise felt several slender ligatures across my body, from my arm-pits to my thighs. I could only look upwards, the sun began to grow hot, and the light offended my eyes. I heard a confused noise about me, but in the posture I lay, could see nothing except the sky. In a little time I felt something alive moving on my left leg, which ad-

> vancing gently forward, over my breast, came almost to my chin; when bending my eyes downward as much as I could, I perceived it to be a human creature not six inches high, with a bow and arrow in his hands, and a quiver at his back.

This is narrative, pure and simple, "as unobstructed as a fable." Read continues:

> But Swift did more than preserve the English idiom; he purified it. It came to him chiefly in the form of the English Bible, as an instinctive mode of expression—direct because it was simple and unconscious, powerful because it was *felt*. Swift accepted it for these simple virtues, but he made it the instrument of his mighty intelligence; and Swift's greatness consists in this fact, more than in anything else, that however deep his insight, his mode of expression remained simple, and single, and clearly comprehensible.

Fielding's style is often as direct and simple as Swift's, but eighteenth-century narrative style does not always exhibit these virtues. Read says:

> The eighteenth-century narrative . . . is interspersed with the author's commentary, his side glances and quizzings, his "philosophical reflections, the like not to be found in any French romance," and eventually, as in the case of Sterne, with any idea that comes into the author's head. This all makes for a certain density of interest, a charm, and even, we must admit, for a higher type of literary art. But the type is only higher in virtue of being

> different; it is no longer in the same category. It has lost unity of action, economy and concreteness,—all the essentials that have been laid down for good narrative prose, which is the prose of action, not of meditation.

As the result of the eighteenth-century novelist's "side glances, quizzings and philosophical reflections," English fiction lost the directness and concreteness that characterized the work of Swift and Defoe. Jane Austen's style is an example of this privation. It has an admirable concreteness but its chief characteristics are those of the essayist. It is well suited to descriptions of landscape, adapts itself beautifully to ironic comments, and is adequate for the rendering of ordinary happenings, but as Read points out, "becomes almost ludicrous" under the strain of out-of-the-way events.

In *Persuasion,* for instance, a young lady, instead of walking down a flight of stairs the way her sisters and friends are doing, insists on being "jumped" down them by Captain Wentworth:

> She was safely down, and instantly, to show her enjoyment, ran up the steps to be jumped down again. He advised her against it, thought the jar too great; but no, he reasoned and talked in vain; she smiled and said, "I am determined I will." He put out his hands; she was precipitate by half a second; she fell on the pavement on the lower Cobb, and was taken up lifeless.
>
> There was no wound, no blood, no visible bruise; but her eyes were closed, she breathed not, her face was like

> death. The horror of that moment to all who stood around!
>
> Captain Wentworth, who had caught her up, knelt with her in his arms, looking on her with a face as pallid as her own, in an agony of silence. "She is dead! she is dead!" screamed Mary, catching hold of her husband, and contributing with his own horror to make him immovable; and in another moment Henrietta, sinking under the conviction, lost her senses too, and would have fallen on the steps but for Captain Benwick and Anne, who caught and supported her between them.
>
> "Is there no one to help me?" were the first words which burst from Captain Wentworth in a tone of despair, and as if all his own strength were gone.

One could hardly blame Captain Wentworth if he too were "sinking under the conviction." Not only is he surrounded by fainting ladies but his creator, too, seems to be letting him down a little.

Read compares this passage with a passage from Emily Brontë's *Wuthering Heights,* in which, as he points out, the style, though equally simple has an emotional intensity which "compels the expression to economy, directness and speed":

> The following evening was very wet, indeed it poured down till day-dawn; and, as I took my morning walk round the house, I observed the master's window swinging open, and the rain driving straight in. He cannot be in bed, I thought: those showers will drench him

through. He must either be up or out. But I'll make no more ado, I'll go boldly and look.

Having succeeded in obtaining entrance with another key, I ran to enclose the panels, for the chamber was vacant; quickly pushing them aside, I peeped in. Mr. Heathcliff was there—laid on his back. His eyes met mine so keen and fierce, I started; and then he seemed to smile. I could not think him dead: but his face and throat were washed with rain; the bed-clothes dripped, and he was perfectly still. The lattice, flapping to and fro, had grazed one hand that rested on the sill; no blood trickled from the broken skin, and when I put my fingers to it, I could doubt no more: he was dead and stark!

I hasped the window; I combed his long black hair from his forehead; I tried to close his eyes: to extinguish, if possible, that frightful, life-like gaze of exaltation before anyone else beheld it. They would not shut: they seemed to sneer at my attempts, and his parted lips and sharp white teeth sneered too!

Read holds that with the Brontës a new vitality and stricter realism came into English fiction; "It was a return to Swift and Defoe or rather, to the fount of even these writers, for we know that the Bible was the most considerable literary influence in Emily Brontë's life. In prose fiction there has been since the middle of the last century no general lapse from this original English idiom among writers of distinction."

I think that we find a notable example of a lapse from "this original English idiom" in the work of Henry James.

Another English writer, himself a considerable stylist, has said something about Swift which sheds light also on James. Dr. Johnson, in his acknowledgment of the same qualities in Swift which Read has held up to our admiration, pays him, seemingly, a reluctant tribute: "The rogue never hazards a metaphor!" He means by that, I suppose, that Swift knew better than most writers the dangers involved in the use of metaphors. A metaphor is, after all, a vehicle of transportation (a transference of names or qualities) from one subject to another through similarities, according to Aristotle's definition. It is a vehicle which transports us into the upper ether and it must be carefully handled or there will be a crash. An airplane "taxis" a while before it leaves the ground. So does a well-constructed metaphor. But Swift did not have to use that vehicle of transportation in his fiction. He kept too close to the ground; after all, he shares his popularity as a teller of tales with Defoe. Henry James was after bigger—and higher-flying—game than either of them.

Although he was certainly severely handicapped by his lack of competence as a prose stylist, we may observe in his case the spectacle that so often astonishes us in the life of a great man: the turning of what seems an almost insuperable obstacle into a point of vantage. His imagination, blocked, as it were, at one outlet, exploded in the dazzling metaphors which shed their radiance over all his work. It is possible that the very awkwardness, the turgidity, of his style makes his metaphors glow more brightly. His characters seem to move in a sort of Rembrandtesque chiaroscuro until the metaphor flashes on the scene a light so brilliant that we perceive things it seems no other light could reveal.

James, possibly out of his necessity, became a forerunner of a distinct trend in fiction. Swift may have been able to avoid metaphors but the modern fiction writer does not seem to be able to do so. The nineteenth century, which saw the rise of industrialism in the social order, of materialism in philosophy, of skepticism in religion, also produced Symbolism. Many of the finest stories of our time, while solidly grounded in Naturalism, are also built on a metaphor, and have some great controlling image. The snow in Joyce's story "The Dead" enters the story as a little round patch on the toe of a man's overshoe and swells and swells until it takes in the whole city and the whole country and, finally, heaven and hell.

The characteristic literary trend of our times is a fusion of Naturalism and Symbolism. Among fiction writers perhaps the greatest exponents of this method are James Joyce and Henry James. Baudelaire foretold their achievements in his remarkable sonnet, *Correspondances.*

La Nature est un temple où des vivants piliers
Laissent parfois sortir des confuses paroles;
L'homme y passe à travers des forêts de symboles
Qui l'observent avec des regards familiers.
Comme de longs échos qui de loin se confondent
Dans une ténébreuse et profonde unité,
Vaste comme la nuit et comme la clarté,
Les parfums, les couleurs et les sons se répondent.

Il est des parfums frais comme des chairs d'enfants,
Doux comme les haut-bois, verts comme les prairies,
—Et d'autres, corrompus, riches et triomphants,
Ayant l'expansion des choses infinies,
Comme l'ambre, le musc, le benjoin, et l'encens,
Qui chantent les transports de l'esprit et des sens.

We see the temple, with its living pillars, we hear the "confused words" that come from the pillars. Man wanders in a *forest of symbols.* He does not quite understand what the pillars are saying to him, but he has seen them before; they "watch him with a familiar look." Baudelaire's sonnet resolves itself as neatly as any novel or play into its component parts of Complication and Resolution. The Complication is man's effort to find out what the pillars are saying to him. Baudelaire resolves the Complication by means of a series of similes which, in the end, combine to form the metaphor which will transport us to the level of symbolic action. He first tells us what the "familiar looks" are like: "long, distant echoes" which merge into a shadowy and profound oneness, vast as darkness and as light. He then tells us what the "familiar looks" *are:* smells, colors, and sounds, the evidences of the five senses. He further particularizes them: some are as fresh as the flesh of infants; others are like flesh that is on the point of decaying. But they all have the "expansion of infinite things," like the gifts which the Magi brought the infant Christ, which were valued both for themselves and for their symbolic significance. These "familiar looks," the things by which we are surrounded every day, "sing the transports of the spirit and the senses"—that is, they are able to lift us from the natural level to the supernatural level.

It is interesting—if depressing—to watch another great imaginative writer wrestling with the problem of the "controlling image." Hawthorne, as a craftsman, had at his command only the outmoded Gothic romance as the vehicle for his genius. When he came back from England and Italy a few years before his death, he retired to the squat, ugly work tower he had built onto his house, "The Wayside," and stayed there until the week of his death, wrestling, unsuccessfully, with the problem that James and Joyce and Baudelaire succeeded in solving. He made several drafts and numberless preparatory sketches for *Septimius Felton* and *Dr. Grimshawe's Secret,* but the stories wouldn't move. Dr. Grimshawe is an aged man whom the hero finds imprisoned in a secret chamber. He seems to be a man who can never die. At least that is the way he strikes the hero, Redclyffe. But why is he the way he is? Hawthorne could never decide just what his secret was. He could not lay hold of the image that would have controlled and directed the action of his story, as the snow controls and directs the action in "The Dead." He did not have at his command Flaubert's method of achieving verisimilitude through the use of concrete details. He had for an engine to hoist him off the ground only the mechanics of the Gothic romance, and it was outworn. His engine wouldn't do what he wanted it to do, wouldn't take him where he wanted to go. Hawthorne kept voluminous notebooks during most of his writing life. Here is the long, sad, colloquy he had with himself in his lonely tower:

> The life is not yet breathed into this plot, after all my galvanic efforts. . . . The Lord of Braithwaite Hall shall be a wretched, dissipated, dishonourable fellow. . . . Something monstrous he shall be, yet within nature and romantic probability—hard conditions! . . . A murderer—'twon't do at all. A Mahometan—pish! Nothing mean must he be, but as wicked as you please. Shall he be preternatural? Not without a plausible explanation. What natural horror is there? A monkey? A Frankenstein? A man of straw? A man wihout a heart, made of machinery? Nonsense! A resurrection man? What—what? What? A cannibal? A ghoul? A vampire? A man who lives by sucking the blood of the young and beautiful? . . . Now for it! How? At any rate, he must have dreadful designs on Elsie—dreadful! dreadful! dreadful! . . . Ye Heavens! A man with a mortal disease? A leprosy? A eunuch? A cork leg? A golden touch? A Cagliostro? This wretched man! A crossing sweeper? A bootblack? . . . It can't be. . . . 'Twon't do. . . . What habit can he have? Perhaps of having a young child, fricasseed, served up to him for breakfast every morning. . . . Do not stick at any strangeness, or preternaturality; it can be softened down to any extent, however wild in its first conception. . . . Alas, me . . . how? how? how? . . . Pshaw, this wretched man still. . . . All this just amounts to nothing. . . . How can I get out of this mess? The devil knows. I don't.

Hawthorne and James each suffered from a severe handicap—Hawthorne in not having at hand and apparently not being able to devise a suitable vehicle for his genius, James in not having undergone in youth the kind of discipline which is the usual preparation for a good prose style. Yet each of them succeeded through his genius in transcending his handicap, indeed in turning it in some cases to his advantage. But not every novelist is capable of the brilliant metaphors which illuminate their works. The novelist may be a poet in the deepest sense, but he is nevertheless condemned to write in prose. The sentence is still his unit of expression and its various qualities are determined by a right sense of this unity. If a novel is really "written," the *shape* of its sentences—their length, their balance, their cadences—will have a great deal to do with the reader's reaction to the work.

Paradoxically, we find in a set of nonsense verses an example of tonal effects which we might find in a well-written novel. "This was the poem that Alice read," in Lewis Carroll's *Through the Looking-Glass:*

Jabberwocky

'Twas brillig, and the slithy toves
   Did gyre and gimble in the wabe:
All mimsy were the borogoves,
   And the mome raths outgrabe.

"Beware the Jabberwock, my son!
   The jaws that bite, the claws that catch!
Beware the Jubjub bird, and shun
   The frumious Bandersnatch!"

He took his vorpal sword in hand:
  Long time the manxome foe he sought—
So rested he by the Tumtum tree,
  And stood a while in thought.

And, as in uffish thought he stood,
  The Jabberwock, with eyes of flame,
Came whiffing through the tulgey wood,
  And burbled as it came!

One, two! One, two! And through and through
  The vorpal blade went snicker-snack!
He left it dead, and with its head
  He went galumphing back. . . .

The story is of a conflict—a conflict which is to the death. It begins at a time of day which the author calls "brillig." The short-"i" vowel has a light, pleasant sound. Its use here tells us that things are going to turn out well. The author would have prepared us for another ending by using a heavier vowel—" 'Twas brooling" or even "brawllig." We surmise that the conflict is serious from the fact that the slithy *toves* do gyre and gimble in the *wabe.* If the conflict were less serious slithy *tives* might gyre and gimble in the *web* and the *borogoves* might be *birogives* and the *mome raths* would certainly not *outgrabe* and might even be *mam riths.* Similarly, the hero might take in hand, instead of his vorpal blade, a *virpal* blade and rest beneath the shade of the *Timtim* tree instead of the Tumtum tree. The enemy whom he was seeking might be a *minxim* foe, instead of a manxome, all of which would make the conflict less serious than it was. However, all turns out well in the end. The hero subdues his foe—in a highly onomatopoeic struggle—and goes *galumphing* back to a father who exclaims, "Oh, frabjous day! Callooh, callay!" instead of crying out, "Oh, frobejous morn, colloe, collorn!" as he might have if his son had been victim instead of victor.

Chapter Ten

The Decline of the Hero

There is only one true subject for fiction, as every folk tale or fairy tale or good novel shows us: the adventures of a hero or heroine—that is, the story of what happened to some man or woman who, through answering the call to the adventure which constitutes the action of the story, comes to stand out from his or her fellows as a remarkable person. If the person in question does not answer the call to this particular adventure he or she fails to qualify as a hero—and there is no story.

The essential characteristics of the hero remain the same through the ages. Nevertheless he appears before us in myriad guises and almost every age has a favorite hero—that is, a man who in his person seems to unite and portray certain trends of that age.

Thackeray said that *Tom Jones* was the "last book in which an English novelist was allowed to depict a man." He meant by that, I take it, a "natural man." Fielding was not obliged to take into account considerations of propriety which weighed more and more heavily on the novelist as Victorian conventions exerted a stronger and stronger strangle-hold on the creative gift.

Thackeray is probably right. Tom Jones is, certainly, a natural man. Fielding makes no bones about his vices.

All the members of Squire Allworthy's family agree that he was "born to be hanged," which is what people have been saying for centuries about any lively, courageous boy. Tom, before he was ten years old, had been convicted of three robberies: fruit out of an orchard, a duck out of a farmyard, and a ball out of the pocket of a sanctimonious prig. "Nevertheless," Fielding says, "Tom, bad as he is, must serve for the hero of this history." And he does serve as a hero magnificently as generations of readers have testified.

What makes Tom a hero? What makes any man a hero? Is it not overcoming obstacles which to the ordinary man would appear insuperable? The thing that distinguishes the Labors of Hercules from the labors you and I perform every day is their seeming impossibility. Hercules was the strongest man that ever lived, but even he couldn't have accomplished them without help. The hero of myth or legend usually has help in accomplishing his feats of strength or skill; often it is supernatural help. A dwarf will spring up beside his stirrup and give him a ring which he is to present as a talisman to the guardian of the palace in which the princess lies sleeping, or an old witch-woman will emerge from a wood and whisper into his ear the words that will unlock the magic portal.

Tom bears a strong resemblance to these legendary heroes. He is not found in a basket in the bulrushes, like Moses, but between the sheets of his prospective foster-father's bed as that good gentleman is on the point of stepping into bed. He recommends himself to Squire Allworthy's attention in the way in which heroes have always recommended themselves, by what Fielding calls "the beauty of innocence." This quality—a kind of incandescent innocence—goes with Tom all through his life. After he becomes a young man Fielding speaks of it as a kind of sweetness of nature which makes everybody love him—unless, as in the case of his foster-father, Squire Allworthy, their minds have been poisoned against him by wicked people like Tom's foster-brother. These wicked people are, of course, a great trial, but where would the fiction writer be without them? He wouldn't have a story if there were no vice for virtue to triumph over.

Tom triumphs. He is every inch a hero. But he is also one of the most natural men that ever lived. His virtues and his vices spring from the same source, a lively interest in the opposite sex. Tom became the father of an illegitimate child when he was still in his teens, and he is also the victim of an overmastering passion for Squire Western's daughter Sophia—"the incomparable Sophia," as her creator calls her.

Tom is in love with Sophia; there is no doubt of that. But he has a regrettable habit of jumping into bed with other women. One of the best scenes in the book, deservedly the most famous, is the evening when Mr. Allworthy, whose life has been despaired of, suddenly takes a turn for the better. Tom is so overjoyed that he drinks a great many bumpers to the doctor's health.

> Jones [says Fielding] had naturally violent animal spirits: these being set on float and augmented by the spirit of wine, produced the most extravagant effects.

> He kissed the doctor, and embraced him with the most passionate endearments; swearing that next to Mr. Allworthy himself, he loved him of all men living. "Doctor," added he, "you deserve a statue to be erected to you at the public expense, for having preserved a man, who is not only the darling of all good men who know him, but a blessing to society, the glory of his country and an honour to human nature. D——n me if I don't love him better than my own soul."
>
> "More shame for you," cries Thwackum [the schoolmaster].

Tom, after having looked on Thwackum with disdain, goes for a walk in what Fielding calls a "delicious grove" to cool his spirits off a bit before attending his foster-father. It is a pleasant evening in the latter end of June and "in this scene, so sweetly accommodated to love," as Fielding puts it, Tom falls to meditating on his dear Sophia. He throws himself on the ground beside a gently murmuring brook and cries out:

> "O Sophia, would Heaven give thee to my arms, how blest would be my condition! Curst be that fortune which sets a distance between us. Was I but possessed of thee, one only suit of rags thy whole estate, is there a man on earth whom I would envy! How contemptible would the brightest Circassian beauty, dressed in all the jewels of the Indies, appear to my eyes! But why do I mention another woman? Could I think my eyes capable of looking at any other with tenderness, these hands should tear them from my head. . . ."

He goes on a good bit after that, as you will remember, and then decides to carve Sophia's name on every tree in the grove, but starting up, penknife in hand, encounters not, as Fielding says,

> a Circassian maid richly and elegantly attired for the grand Signior's seraglio. No; without a gown, in a shift that was somewhat of the coarsest, and none of the cleanest, bedewed likewise with some odoriferous effluvia, the produce of the day's labour, with a pitchfork in her hand, Molly Seagrim approached. Our hero had his penknife in his hand, which he had drawn for the beforementioned purpose of carving on the bark; when the girl coming near him, cried out with a smile, "You don't intend to kill me, squire, I hope?"—"Why should you think I would kill you?" answered Jones.—"Nay," replied she, "after your cruel usage of me when I saw you last, killing me would perhaps be too great kindness for me to expect."

Tom, being the putative father of Molly's illegitimate child and also one of the kindest men that ever lived, feels that he must disabuse the poor girl of the notion that he wishes her any harm, and what Fielding calls "a parley" ensues, which, he says, he does not feel obliged to relate and therefore omits. "It is sufficient," he says, "that it lasted a full quarter of an hour, at the conclusion of which they retired into the thickest part of the grove."

The reader, who is in a better situation to keep a lookout than Tom, is not surprised when Thwackum the schoolmaster and Blifil, Tom's wicked foster-brother, come past. Blifil tells the schoolmaster that he is certain he had seen "a fellow and a wench retire together among the bushes" and doubts not that "it is with some wicked purpose." Molly escapes by crawling away through the bushes, but poor Tom is captured and as a result of this evening's affair loses Squire Allworthy's favor and is sent out in the world to shift for himself.

Tom does not seem to learn much from adversity, for we find him again and again in situations as compromising as his meeting with Molly in the grove. For when the "incomparable Sophia," who is also impelled by love to leave home and wander, arrives at a certain inn, she finds Tom there too, involved with Mrs. Waters, a lady of light virtue. Nobody can blame Sophia for refusing to see Tom and leaving the inn as soon as possible, but it is interesting to ascertain just how Tom came to make the acquaintance of Mrs. Waters. Tom tells the mysterious recluse, "The Man of the Hill," that he wants to walk to a certain eminence in order to enjoy the view. When he arrives at the top of the hill he stands for some minutes with his eyes fixed on the south. When his companion asks him what he is looking at he says with a sigh that he is endeavoring to trace his own journey thither. The Man of the Hill, who in his time has been a man of the world, knows a lover when he sees one, and tells Tom that he suspects from his sighing that he is also thinking of something that "you love better than your own home, or I am mistaken." Tom admits that this is the case.

They now walked to that part of the hill which looks to the north-west, and which hangs over a vast and extensive wood. Here they were no sooner arrived than they heard at a distance the most violent screams of a woman, proceeding from the wood below them. Jones listened a moment, and then, without saying a word to his companion (for indeed the occasion seemed sufficiently pressing), ran or rather slid, down the hill, and, without the least apprehension or concern for his own safety, made directly to the thicket whence the sound had issued.

He had not entered far into the wood before he beheld a most shocking sight indeed, a woman stripped half naked, under the hands of a ruffian, who had put his garter round her neck, and was endeavouring to draw her up to a tree. Jones asked no questions at this interval, but fell instantly upon the villain, and made such good use of his trusty oaken stick that he laid him sprawling on the ground before he could defend himself, indeed almost before he knew he was attacked; nor did he cease the prosecution of his blows till the woman herself begged him to forbear, saying, she believed he had sufficiently done his business.

The poor wretch then fell upon her knees to Jones, and gave him a thousand thanks for her deliverance. He presently lifted her up, and told her he was highly pleased with the extraordinary accident which had sent him thither for her relief, where it was so improbable she should find any; adding that Heaven seemed to have designed him as the happy instrument of her protection. "Nay," answered she, "I could almost conceive you to be some good angel; and, to say the truth, you look

> more like an angel than a man in my eye." Indeed he was a charming figure; and if a very fine person, and a most comely set of features, adorned with youth, health, strength, freshness, spirit, and good-nature, can make a man resemble an angel, he certainly had that resemblance.

Tom may look like an angel but he does not act like one that evening. He is in bed with Mrs. Waters at the inn to which he has conducted her when the peerless Sophia arrives at that same inn.

Mrs. Waters may perhaps be regarded as the prototype of all light ladies, just as the peerless Sophia plays the role of Beatrice to Tom's Dante—if one can think of Tom as a poet. But I think that the way in which Tom makes Mrs. Waters' acquaintance is important in his history. He meets her by playing the role of a knight-errant, going to rescue a woman in distress. Tom is as blundering a hero as can be found in all literature. At times he is so stupid that we almost wash our hands of him, but he is nevertheless always the hero. No matter how low his own fortunes are he is always ready to drop whatever he is doing to help somebody whose fortunes are lower than his own. His ear seems always keyed to the cry of distress. If he hears someone cry out for help he doesn't stop to consider whether the person who is crying out is worthy of help or how much the rescue may cost him. He obeys an impulse which seems to stem from an overflowing of spirit. He is a hero, just as Sophia is a heroine, and we are all glad to find them at the end of the book married and living happily.

Fielding intersperses the action of his novel throughout with chapters of pure reflection—on almost any subject that comes into his head. In one of these chapters he discusses the passion of love in the light of "that modern doctrine, by which certain philosophers, among many other wonderful discoveries, pretend to have found out that there is no such passion in the human breast," and he concludes that this passion, as it manifests itself in the relations between men and women, is the only subject that interests him to write about. He says:

> Examine your heart, my good reader, and resolve whether you do believe these matters with me. If you do, you may now proceed to their exemplification in the following pages: if you do not, you have, I assure you, already read more than you have understood; and it would be wiser to pursue your business, or your pleasures (such as they are), than to throw away any more of your time in reading what you can neither taste nor comprehend. To treat of the effects of love to you, must be as absurd as to discourse on colours to a man born blind; since possibly your idea of love may be absurd as that which we are told such blind man once entertained of the colour scarlet; that colour seemed to him to be very much like the sound of a trumpet: and love probably may, in your opinion, very greatly resemble a dish of soup or a sirloin of roast-beef.

The imagination of a great fiction writer is a mysterious region. He himself, perhaps, hardly understands what goes on there. Fielding has not only written an able defense of his own kind of writing but has inadvertently prophesied the kind of novel that will be written if novelists seek other subjects than love as the material on which to base their fictions. *Tom Jones* was published in 1749. It is interesting to compare this great English novel with a novel written by a Frenchman and translated into English in 1947. Jean Paul Sartre's *Age of Reason*[1] reads like a fulfillment of Fielding's prophecy. In *Tom Jones* the passion of love between men and women is the motivating force of the action. In *Age of Reason,* heterosexual love appears in quite another guise. Tom Jones is so lively—and lusty—that he will leap out of bed in the middle of the night to answer a cry of distress from a woman he has never seen. Sartre's characters are concerned with one thing: existence. They are all either very anxious to convince themselves or to be convinced that they do exist, or, as in the case of the hero, Mathieu Delarue, in *Age of Reason,* anxious to convince themselves that they don't exist. None of his heroes would ever leap out of bed in the middle of the night to answer the cry of distress of an unknown woman. They have a hard enough time getting themselves into bed in the first place.

Delarue, a professor in the Sorbonne, is walking up the rue Vercingetorix in the Latin Quarter on his way to visit his mistress Marcelle when we first catch sight of him. Like many professors, Mathieu sometimes yearns to be a man of action. He wanted to go and fight in Spain but never brought himself to take the step. He is accosted by a vagrant who asks him for a franc or two. Mathieu gives him five francs and tells him he doesn't care whether he uses it for food or drink. The vagrant is affected by this recognition of their common humanity and tells him he wants to give *him* something in return and he pulls out of his pocket a green stamp. He is offended when Mathieu simply thanks him and thrusts it into his pocket. "Ah, but look," he says, "it's—it's Madrid." And then he says, "I wanted to get there, and that's the truth. But it couldn't be fixed." He then asks Delarue to have a drink with him but Delarue declines.

As he goes on his way, Delarue reflects that he and the vagrant are in the same situation in that each of them had a chance to do something out of the ordinary. He, too, had wanted to go and fight in Spain, but "it couldn't be fixed." A railway whistle, emblem of journeys, blows. He tells himself that he is getting old and continues on his way to visit his mistress Marcelle.

One envies Sophia Western. It must be wonderful to be so beautiful that everybody gasps when you enter a room, or so virtuous that nobody has a word to say against you, but one is inclined to pity Sartre's heroine. Sophia, for all she is the daughter of a country squire, gets around, goes out in London society under the chaperonage of her aunt Western and wanders over the country companioned only by her maid Honour. But poor Marcelle, as far as her creator reports, never leaves her bedroom. She sits there, he says, looking "like a great porcelain vase." The room is a dim pink and Mathieu always feels as if he were entering a seashell when he goes there. He has been visiting his mistress twice a week now for seven years but he can hardly be described as an eager lover.

Simone de Beauvoir has named her book *The Second Sex;* one is tempted to think of poor Marcelle as a representative of some sex newly originated, a woman who, in order to get her rights, has given up all her prerogatives. Both Marcelle and Mathieu consider marriage degrading and have never entertained the idea of regularizing their union. But Marcelle finds it dull to sit alone in her dim-pink room and on one occasion suggests that her lover take her out to dinner. He reflects and says that he couldn't possibly make it before fall—it is now early summer—and adds that he doesn't really think she'd enjoy it, anyhow. Marcelle's disposition hasn't improved under this treatment and when he tells her about the adventure of the stamp and says that the vagrant wanted to stand him a drink she asks him why he didn't accept and expresses the opinion that his refusal of the offer is "symptomatic." "It's that same lucidity you fuss about so much. You're so absurdly afraid of being your own dupe, my poor boy, that you would back out of the finest adventure in the world rather than risk telling a lie."

Mathieu is annoyed by this but has to admit to himself that she is right. He thinks of lucidity "as the inner meaning of their love. . . . He could not love Marcelle save in complete lucidity; she was his lucidity embodied, his comrade, his witness, his counselor, and his critic."

He is still more annoyed when she comments on his taste for self-analysis. He indulges in self-analysis, she says, because it helps him to get rid of himself. ". . . That's the attitude you prefer. When you look at yourself, you imagine you aren't what you see, you imagine you are nothing. That is your ideal: you want to be nothing."

"To be nothing," Mathieu repeats. "No. . . . Listen. . . . I recognize no allegiance except to myself."

"Yes," she says, "you want to be free. Absolutely free. It's your vice."

"It's not a vice," he replies. "What else can a man do? If I didn't try to assume responsibility for my own existence, it would seem utterly absurd to go on existing."

A look of "smiling obstinacy" now comes over Marcelle's face. It develops that her lover may have to assume responsibility for another existence. She has just found out that she is going to have a child. Tom Jones became a father in his teens—you remember that affair with Molly Seagrim, the daughter of Black George the gamekeeper—a highly regrettable affair, as Tom himself is the first person to admit. But it seems that the country-bred boy of eighteen is better adjusted, as the psychiatrists call it, to the facts of life than the thirty-four-year-old professor at the Sorbonne. Tom isn't particularly surprised when he finds that Moll is about to have a child and with no ado assumes the responsibility for both child and mother. Sartre's hero finds the idea of becoming a father grotesque, but he too shoulders his responsibilities—in Existentialist fashion—and marches grimly off in search of a doctor who will extricate Marcelle from her predicament.

The search for the doctor constitutes a large part of the action of the story. The doctor, when found, demands a sum of money larger than Mathieu can raise. Mathieu finally steals it, but before he does that there are many telephone calls, visits to friends, and many late sessions in cafés. One of his companions during his frenzied search is one of his female students, a young Russian girl named Ivich Serguine with whom he is half in love. Ivich is trying to get a doctorate in medicine but so far has been handicapped by her habit of always turning up intoxicated when it is time for her to take an examination. She has no great ambition to be a doctor, nor any interest in her work. Her real ambition is to feel—to feel emotion of some kind, she doesn't much care what. During one of the sessions in a café she takes up her brother's knife and slashes her hand. Mathieu takes the knife from her and slashes his hand, too. They press their wounded palms together and feel a kind of communion they have never known before. The high point of their relationship may be said to come when they are having their wounds bound up by a kindly lavatory attendant. Ivich actually promises Mathieu that tomorrow she will do her hair the way he has always wanted to see it, drawn back so that her face is clearly visible, instead of half-obscured by a mass of curls, but the next afternoon when he suspends the search for the money long enough to take her to a museum she has expressed a desire to visit, she is wearing her hair in the fashion he dislikes.

Marcelle, meanwhile, is secretly receiving visits from another friend, Daniel Lalique. Daniel, who is also a friend of Mathieu's, has been visiting her for months, but Mathieu does not know that. Daniel likes that dim-pink room of Marcelle's even less than Mathieu. In fact, after each visit to Marcelle, he always has a bad attack of a respiratory trouble to which he is subject, but he keeps visiting her just the same. He is attracted to Marcelle because she is Mathieu's mistress. He hates and envies Mathieu and when he finds out that Marcelle is pregnant he decides that he will put the lovers' plight to a use which he himself realizes as truly diabolical. He will wreck Mathieu's life by, as it were, forcing him to marry Marcelle, forcing him to become what Mathieu has always refused to become: an ordinary man, with an ordinary man's cares and duties. Daniel has always been jealous of Mathieu's influence over his students. "I wonder if he will have any disciples now," he muses. "A family man won't be quite so popular in such a part."

But both Marcelle and Mathieu prove to be more resistent to his experiment than he had foreseen. Marcelle desperately wants to bear her child, but she is not prepared to marry an unwilling Mathieu in order to do it. They quarrel more fiercely than they have ever quarreled before. Mathieu, after flinging the money he has stolen down before her, rushes out of the house and goes on a round of the cafés with Ivich. Ivich has at last succeeded in mustering an emotion: she is in despair over having failed in her examinations, for that means that she will have to go home and live with her family, a fate she regards as extinction. She has treated Mathieu with coldness up to this time but now is a little kinder to him.

> It was the same face she turned towards him on the previous evening, when the lavatory dame was bandaging her hand. He eyed her dubiously, he felt his desire revive.

> That sad and resigned desire which was a desire *for nothing.* He took her arm, he felt the cool flesh beneath his fingers. And he said:
>
> "I — you . . ."

This not very impassioned love scene is interrupted when the door opens and Lola, the woman from whom Mathieu has stolen the five thousand francs, bursts into the room. Lola is under the impression that her young lover, Boris, has stolen the money. Mathieu tells her that it was not Boris but he who took it. When Ivich learns for what purpose he took the money she leaves. The author says that Mathieu "heard with relief the light patter of her feet" in the hall. And, indeed, poor Mathieu has enough on his hands without her, for while he is still trying to persuade Lola that it was he and not Boris who took the money, Daniel comes in and hands Lola an envelope containing the five thousand francs which, he assures her and Mathieu, "are no longer needed." Lola looks at Mathieu with "an immense astonishment and a sort of curiosity," then she too leaves. Mathieu is left confronting Daniel, who informs him that he and Marcelle are going to be married.

Mathieu leaps to the conclusion that Daniel has all along been Marcelle's lover. Daniel tells him that that is "not a bad guess. Just what would suit your book, eh? No, my dear fellow, you haven't even that excuse." He then informs Mathieu that he is homosexual. Mathieu asks him why, in that case, he is marrying Marcelle.

Daniel replies, "Well, I—I wanted to see the effect it

would produce on a fellow like you. Also, now that there's someone who *knows,* I—I shall perhaps succeed in believing it. . . . Does it surprise you? Does it upset your conception of inverts?"

"Don't throw your weight about," Mathieu says. . . . "There's no need to do that for my benefit. You are disgusted with yourself, I suppose, but not more so than I am with myself, there's nothing much to choose between us. Besides," he adds after a moment's reflection, "that's why you tell me all this. It must be easier to confess to a derelict like me; and you get the advantage of the confession just the same."

Daniel tells him that he is a "sly little devil."

Mathieu suddenly feels that he cannot let Marcelle marry this man and calls her up and shouts into the telephone, "Marcelle, I want to marry you," but hears nothing but a brief silence and then a yapping sound at the end of the line and a concluding click of the receiver, and he gives up the attempt.

Daniel tells him not to worry about Marcelle, that it is a well-known fact that homosexuals often make the best husbands. He then reveals his real reason for wanting to marry Marcelle and adopt the child that is to be born. Homosexuals who accept the fact that they are homosexuals are, he says, "dead men. Their very sense of shame has killed them. I don't want to die that sort of death." He looks at Mathieu now without hatred and says quietly, "I have accepted myself only too thoroughly, I know myself inside out." Mathieu says abruptly, "I wish I were in your place."

Daniel shrugs his shoulders and tells him that in this affair he, Mathieu, has been "the winner all around. You are free."

Mathieu shakes his head. "It isn't by giving up a woman that a man is free," he says. . . . "The truth is I gave Marcelle up for nothing. For nothing," he repeats. "In all this affair I have been a sort of embodied refusal, a negation."

He then considers Daniel's situation and envies him. "He has *acted,*" he thinks, "and now he can't go back; it must seem strange to him to feel behind an unknown act which he has already almost ceased to understand and which will turn his life upside down. All I do, I do for *nothing*. It might be said that I am robbed of the consequences of my acts; everything happens as though I could always play my strokes again. I don't know what I would give to do something irrevocable."

"I should like to be six months older," Daniel says.

"I wouldn't," Mathieu says. "In six months I shall be the same as I am now."

Daniel leaves him and our hero walks to the window and surveys the blue night sky—and yawns.

"I remain alone," he reflects. He had said to himself last evening, "If only Marcelle did not exist." But in so doing he deceived himself. "No one has interfered with my freedom," he tells himself. "My life has drained it dry." He shuts the window and turning back into the room, inhales the lingering traces of the scent which Ivich uses and thinks how, when he held her in his arms a few hours ago, he was holding nothing, and he reviews the day of tumult and concludes that it has all been much ado about nothing. "For nothing: this life had been given him for nothing, he was nothing, and yet he would not change." He sits down, takes off his shoes—and yawns again. "It's true," he thinks, "it's really true. I have attained the age of reason."

Joseph Campbell, in a book called *The Hero of a Thousand Faces,* has analyzed a great many stories, among them many legends and fairy tales, with a view to determining the essential nature of the hero. He concludes that the hero, wherever he appears, in whatever age or in what guise, has certain characteristics and is faced always with the same task: the overcoming of evil that good may flourish. In the folk tales and myths evil often takes the form of a dragon or monster. Sometimes, like Perseus, the hero slays the dragon in order to free a maiden whom the dragon has imprisoned. The maiden whom he frees symbolizes in part his own life energies. Mr. Campbell says:

> She is the maiden of the innumerable dragon slayings, the bride abducted by the jealous father, the virgin rescued from the unholy lover. She is the "other portion" of the hero himself—for "each is both": if his stature is that of world monarch she is the world, and if he is a warrior she is fame. She is the image of his destiny which he is to release from the prison of enveloping circumstance. But where he is ignorant of his destiny or deluded by false considerations, no effort on his part will overcome the obstacles.

Tom Jones, after all his ups and downs, attains fame through his marriage to Sophia Western: "There is not a neighbour, a tenant, or a servant who does not gratefully bless the day when Mr. Jones was married to his Sophia." Mathieu Delarue acknowledges no allegiance except to himself ("What else can a man do?" he tells his mistress) and attains "the age of reason," which, in his own mind, he equates with nothingness. His plight is that of many modern heroes of fiction. R. P. Blackmur, in an essay called "The Hero as Disconsolate Chimera," has made some observations which throw considerable light upon the dilemma of this hero:

> In the Middle Ages the characteristic hero was the prince or the soldier, someone in high station, represented by a poet nearly anonymous. The prince or the soldier was the motive of the action. By the Renaissance both the artist and the hero had become somewhat more individualized, the motive and the conscience somewhat obscured. By the eighteenth century the artist was rooted for his inspiration in a relatively fixed national society; his heroes were descendants of the earlier breeds and had fallen in social position—they were the same heroes but were celebrated at a less heroic level. Motive and conscience had become easy. Here is the crisis in this sequence. With the romantic period, when the historical sense came in, a new decision was taken: the artist himself might be a hero, as Byron, Goethe, Hugo were themselves heroes greater than any of the heroes in their works; motive and conscience had got outside the works. But the day of this hero was short, though it has never been forgotten. Except for the virtuosi who did very well, the artist became the hero *manqué,* the *poète maudit,* and

celebrated himself or prototypes of himself in his works. Then with the rise of symbolism and art for art's sake the heroes of a considerable body of work began to be portrayed as artists. The subject of the artist and the special sensibility of the artist began to be the heroic subject and the heroic sensibility which best expressed society itself. The problem of the artist became a version of the problem of man. . . .

This sort of belief is a part of the behavior—it is as deep as that—of a major fraction of the thousands of fresh artists our system throws up every year into fuller isolation and with a more certain end in failure than before.

If Mr. Blackmur is right, the author who celebrates only himself, or prototypes of himself, does not create a work of art, for, as he points out, the hero whose aim is expression, without need of either conscience or motive, is not a real hero and therefore not a fit subject for artistic creation. Heroes don't start out as extraordinary men. They become extraordinary men by performing extraordinary deeds. Mr. Blackmur's "hero of expression" is incapable of the adventures that befall heroes; his energies are absorbed in the task of being, not doing. In the next chapter I should like to discuss the role played by these "disconsolate chimeras" in a world they helped to make.

Chapter Eleven

The Novelist and His World

Years ago, when I was a great deal younger than I am now, I sat in a corner of Gertrude Stein's vast studio on the rue Fleurus and listened—impatiently—while Miss Stein descanted on the nature of her own genius. She said that there had been only four American writers of any consequence—Hawthorne, Emerson, Whitman, and herself. Hawthorne, she said, was the first real American genius. Emerson took up where he left off. Whitman carried on from there. "But the true American genius, the genius which is unique in being able to dispense with experience, comes to its flower in me," she said. "That is why streetcar conductors like to read my work so much. They recognize its Americanism. European writers are handicapped by reality, by experience. . . . Look at poor old Joyce!"

It is sometimes amusing to listen to nonsense but it is irritating to have to listen to nonsense when serious matters are under discussion. I was engaged in writing my first novel when I heard Miss Stein make her pronouncement and I was considerably irritated. As the years go by the feeling has grown rather than diminished. Over and over—sometimes in highly respectable literary circles—I have heard people saying the same kind of thing that Miss Stein was saying that evening and always I am reminded of another formidable literary lady, Margaret Fuller, who was, perhaps, more fortunate than Miss Stein in that she finally, albeit with reluctance, accepted reality in the shape of the universe. We all know what Carlyle said about that.

Miss Stein, in the days when I was admitted to her presence, did not seem to have a Carlyle handy and even then was setting out on the primrose pathway that led to her extinction as an artist. Almost every fiction writer comes upon this primrose path at some time in his career. If he is wise he will heed Carlyle's grim warning and accept such manifestations of reality as come his way. If he ignores the nature of his medium and proceeds on Miss Stein's theory that fiction can be divorced from experience, that is to say, reality, he is likely to fall into a trap that yawns for every writer, a trap so deep that it might almost be called an abyss—deep enough, at any rate, to swallow up the work of a man's whole lifetime. Yvor Winters, in his *Defense of Reason,*[1] has labeled it "The Fallacy of Imitative Form." He says:

> This law of literary aesthetics has never that I know been stated explicitly. It might be thus formulated: Form is expressive invariably of the state of mind of the author; a state of formlessness is legitimate subject matter for literature, and in fact all subject matter, as such, is relatively formless; but the author must endeavor to give form, or meaning, to the formless—in so far as he endeavors that his own state of mind may imitate or approximate the matter, he is surrendering to the matter instead of mastering it. Form, in so far as it endeavors to imitate the formless, destroys itself.

It has remained for Mr. Winters to name this fallacy of imitative form but he is not the first critic to discern its nature. Aristotle, in his *Poetics,* warns us against it when he cites what we nowadays call "a horrible example," the even then long-forgotten author of a poem called "The Heracleidae." This poet—the Thomas Wolfe of his day?—included *all* the adventures of Heracles in his epic poem, thereby failing to achieve any form, whereas Homer, Aristotle points out, used in the *Odyssey* only such of Odysseus' adventures as suited his purpose, a purpose, which, according to Aristotle, was the imitation of an "action" of a certain magnitude—that is, the account of how Odysseus got back to his home in Ithaca after the siege of Troy.

The author who succumbs to the fallacy of destroying form by imitating the formless usually follows one of two paths, which, apparently widely diverging, come, I suspect, to the same end. As we have seen, a certain degree of humility, of self-abasement, is necessary if one is to succeed in reading fiction well. There is a right attitude toward the subject matter of any book for both author and reader. A reader, after he has finished a book, is certainly entitled to make any comments on it or criticisms of it that enter into his head. But if, while he is engaged in the reading of the book, he allows his own opinions or prejudices to come between him and the author's presentation of his subject matter, he is not giving the book the kind of reading it should have or, indeed, the best reading that he himself is capable of. This is asking a great deal of the reader and few readers attain to such detachment, such humility.

Even more is demanded of the author. He, too, must abase himself before his subject matter and his exercise of humility necessarily lasts longer than that of the reader. It is often prolonged almost beyond the powers of human endurance, as Thomas Mann has shown us in his *Death in Venice.* The prologue of that brilliant novella deals with the agonies resulting from the exercise over a long period of years of the successive acts of will and imagination which make up the smooth, apparently effortless public performances of the novelist Gustav von Aschenbach.

In such a situation—the situation which the writer of serious fiction confronts day after day, if not hour after hour, during his whole working life—the artist is tempted to seek an easier way out. If he does succumb to this temptation he will in all probability choose one of two ways. He will either attempt to rise above his subject matter, that is, glorify himself at its expense, or he will fall below it, indulging in a self-deprecation so profound that it prevents his confronting it.

Miss Stein's solution seems to have been to exalt herself above her subject matter. Serious students of her work —and her imaginative gifts were considerable enough to demand serious consideration—cannot but be struck by the contrast between her early and late work. *Three Lives,* for instance, delights by its sharply defined form, but as her work progressed form gave way to mood and the later works are chiefly projections of the author's personality, or, as in the case of *The Autobiography of Alice*

B. Toklas, commentary on or justification of the author's methods.

André Gide is a conspicuous example of another writer who destroys the form of his work by imitating the formless. His failure as a novelist springs, I suspect, from the same source as Miss Stein's, an unwillingness or inability to accept reality—that is, to recognize the existence of a world outside his own consciousness. His way out is, on the surface, very different from Miss Stein's. Instead of self-magnification and self-gratulation, we find his works characterized by timidity, a timidity so excessive that he never really confronts his subject matter, but instead tries to make drama out of his own efforts to escape that necessary and terrible confrontation. I do not know where one can find a better example of the fallacy of imitative form than in the novel generally regarded as his masterpiece, *The Counterfeiters* (*Les Faux Monnayeurs*). The confusion, the double-mindedness which reigned in Gide's life and paralyzed his imagination are faithfully reflected in this, his most ambitious work.

In *The Counterfeiters* he puts into the mouth of Edouard, a would-be novelist, many of his own ideas about the novel as an art form, an art form divorced from experience. Edouard says that he would like "to strip the novel of reality. . . . The novel," he says, "is of all literary genres the *freest,* the most *lawless.* . . . Is it for that very reason, for fear of that very liberty that the novel has always clung to reality with such timidity? . . . The only progress it looks to is to get still nearer to nature. The novel has never known that 'formidable erosion of contours,' as Nietzsche calls it, that deliberate avoidance of life, which gave style to the works of the Greek dramatists, for instance."

This passage seems to me to voice a serious misconception not only of the works of the Greek dramatists—and of the myths on which their plays are based—but a misconception of the nature of the novel as an art form. And indeed Gide, with the double-mindedness which characterized his every act, condemned himself out of the mouth of one of his own characters, who remarks of Edouard's attempt to write a novel, "He'll never finish it. That method of working he described to us seemed to me absurd. A good novel gets itself written more naïvely than that. . . . First of all, one must believe in one's own story—and tell it quite simply. . . . But with an idea-monger there's nothing doing."

I think that a kind of timidity kept Gide from the whole-hearted commitment to his story which every artist must make if he is to have a story, on any level. For Gide attempted to provide against the possibility of failure before he even embarked on his venture, by giving himself, so to speak, an alibi: he made the action of his story subordinate to the telling of it from the start.

He kept a journal while he was writing *The Counterfeiters,* in which he recorded the hopes, the fears, the struggles he went through while attempting to write the book. In one place he said:

> The extreme difficulty I am encountering in making my book progress is perhaps the natural result of an initial

> vice. From time to time I am convinced that the very idea of the book is ridiculous and I come to the point where I no longer understand what I want. Properly speaking, the book has no one single center for my various efforts to converge upon; those efforts center upon two foci, as in an ellipse. On one side, the event, the fact, the external datum; on the other side, the very effort of the novelist to make a book out of it all. The latter is the main subject, the focus that throws the plot off center and leads it towards the imaginative. In short, I see in this note-book in which I am writing the very history of the novel poured into the book in its entirety and forming its principal interest—for the greater irritation of the reader.

Gide, in his journal, thought of himself as resembling Edouard, the would-be novelist, as indeed he does. Another of his leading characters, Count Robert de Passavant, a wealthy Parisian, also writes novels, but his chief interest is the sexual debauchery of young boys. Gide says in *The Counterfeiters:*

> Edouard knew Passavant ill. He was ignorant of one of the chief traits of his character. No one had ever succeeded in catching Passavant out; it was unbearable to him to be worsted. In order not to acknowledge his defeats to himself, he always affected to have desired his fate, and whatever happened to him he pretended that that was what he wished.

This timidity, this conviction of Passavant that he could never amount to much, impels him to a kind of intellectual petty larceny. He is continually stealing other people's ideas and passing them off as his own.

An image of the sea recurs throughout the book. It is first presented in the conversation of Vincent Molinier, a young medical student, who is much interested in natural science. Vincent says to Passavant and his own future mistress, Lady Lillian Griffith:

> "You know, no doubt, that the light of the day does not reach very far down into the sea. Its depths are dark . . . huge gulfs, which for a long time were thought to be uninhabited; then people began dragging them and quantities of strange animals were brought up from these infernal regions—animals that were blind, it was thought. What use would the sense of sight be in the dark? Evidently they had no eyes; they wouldn't, they couldn't have eyes. Nevertheless, on examination, it was found to people's amazement that some of them *had* eyes, and sometimes antennae of extraordinary sensibility into the bargain. Still people doubted and wondered: why eyes with no means of seeing? Eyes that were sensitive—but sensitive to what? . . . And at last it was discovered that each of these animals which people at first insisted were creatures of darkness, gives forth and projects before and around it its *own* light. Each of them shines, illuminates, irradiates. When they were brought up from the depths at night and turned out onto the ship's deck, the darkness blazed. Moving, many-coloured fires, glowing, vibrating, changing—revolving beacon-lamps—sparkling of stars and jewels—a spectacle, say those who saw it, of unparalleled splendour."

Passavant is impressed by what Vincent says. He calls this kind of thing "ideas in the air"—that is, other people's ideas—and helps himself to them freely. So, a few months later, we find Vincent's young brother Olivier, who is off in the mountains on a vacation with the Count, writing to his friend, Bernard Profitendieu, that there is no chance of being bored in Passavant's company, since he has such original ideas. Olivier writes:

> I am trying to persuade him all I can to write about some new theories he has on deep-sea fishes and what he calls "their private lights," which enables them to do without the light of the sun—which he compares to grace and revelation.

In this recurrent image of the sea and its denizens we find, I think, a key to Gide's own dilemma. The image appears again in a letter which Lady Griffith writes Passavant after she has persuaded Vincent to abandon his mistress, Laura Douviers, who is about to have his child, and to go off on a cruise with her on the Prince of Monaco's yacht. She writes Passavant that she "and Vincent" are going to Africa, he to botanize and she to shoot. They have fallen, she says, into the clutches of the demon of adventure.

> He was introduced to us by the demon of boredom whose acquaintance we made on board ship. . . . Ah, *cher!* One must live on a yacht to know what boredom is. In rough weather life is just bearable; one has one's share

of the vessel's agitation. But after Teneriffe, not a breath, not a wrinkle on the sea—the great mirror of my despair.

The sea has always furnished man with images of eternity, of infinity. The poet Hart Crane in one line speaks of the sea as "that great wink of eternity." But Gide and his characters—and I think it is a mark of Gide's failure as a novelist that he and his characters are almost indistinguishable—Gide and his characters, in making the sea glow only with their own "private lights," instead of reflecting some supernatural illumination, cut the sea, immemorial image of infinity, down to their own size and succeed in making it, as Lady Griffith puts it, "the great mirror of their despair."

Gide, unable to turn away from that mirror in which he never seems to confront anything but some aspect of himself, succumbed to the same timidity which afflicted Robert de Passavant. He is so afraid that he will not succeed in the arduous task of contriving the illusion of reality, of creating characters who appear to exist independently of their author, that, like Passavant, he pretends that he desires the hard fate which he foresees. He insists that the journal which Edouard keeps is more important than the action of the story.

The action begins when young Bernard Profitendieu raises the onyx top of a table and discovers a packet of letters which had been written twenty years ago to his mother by a lover whose existence he has not suspected until this moment. He leaps to a conclusion that he has always unconsciously longed to reach: that Monsieur Profitendieu, *le juge d'instruction,* is not his real father. He writes the judge a letter telling him of his discovery and leaves home. But he has no money and is forced to beg a night's lodging of his schoolmate, Olivier Molinier. Olivier has left a side door open for him and he slips up into Olivier's room late at night. Olivier, a sensitive, gifted boy, is much excited over a discovery he has just made: that his older brother, Vincent, has a mistress. He has heard them talking on a landing on the stairs outside his room. The woman who is about to have a child is begging Vincent Molinier not to desert her, but Vincent goes up the stairs and shuts the door, and the woman, after sobbing outside the door for a while, goes away. The two boys discuss Vincent's affair in whispers, taking care not to waken Georges, a younger brother, who sleeps in the same room, and then Olivier goes on to discuss something that interests him just as much: his uncle, Edouard, the novelist, half-brother of his mother, is due to arrive tomorrow.

Edouard, though Olivier does not know it, was once in love with Laura, Vincent's about-to-be-discarded mistress. In the journal which he keeps all through the action Edouard writes:

> Up till now I have never written a line that has not been inspired by her . . . all the skill of my discourse is due only to my constant desire to instruct, to convince, to captivate her. I see nothing, I hear nothing, without asking myself what she would think of it. And I think that if she were not there to give definition to my person-

ality, it would vanish in the excessive vagueness of its contours. It is only round her that I concentrate and define myself.

But a change has come over Edouard in the past few months, a change which he duly notes in his journal. He has concluded that "the influence of love, by a curious action of give and take," has made him and Laura "reciprocally alter their natures."

> "Involuntarily—unconsciously—each one of a pair of lovers fashions himself to meet the other's requirements—endeavours by a continual effort to resemble that idol of himself which is hidden in the other's heart. . . . Whoever really loves abandons sincerity."

In the interest of achieving sincerity, he has persuaded Laura that he and she are not for each other. She dutifully marries an estimable man named Felix Douviers, then contracts tuberculosis. While recuperating from the disease in the mountains, she meets Vincent Molinier, who is there for the same reason, and becomes his mistress. When she finds that she is about to have a child she comes to Paris in the hope that Vincent will help her, since she feels that she cannot go back to her husband in these circumstances.

Gide speaks in one place of the devil circulating through the book now in one disguise, now in another. The book takes its name from the activities of the young "counterfeiters," members of "The Brotherhood of Strong Men," an organization inspired by Robert de Passavant and directed by Strouvilhou, a sinister character who, in turn, has as his tool his schoolboy cousin, Léon Gheridanisol. The members of the Brotherhood wear a yellow ribbon in their buttonholes and are sworn to stop at nothing that the Brotherhood directs them to do. They accomplish a murder before they are disbanded, but their chief activity is the circulation of counterfeit coins.

Strouvilhou says to Léon:

> "The kids we want, you see, are those who come of good families, because then if rumours get about, their parents will do all they can to stifle them. Only with this system of selling the coins one by one, they get into circulation too slowly. I've got fifty-two boxes containing twenty coins each, to dispose of. They must be sold for twenty francs a box; but not to anyone, you understand. The best thing would be to form an association to which no one should be admitted who didn't furnish pledges. The kids must be made to compromise themselves, and hand over something or other which will give us a hold over their parents. Before letting them have the coins, they must be made to understand that—oh, without frightening them. One must never frighten children. You told me Molinier's father was a magistrate? Good. And Adamanti's father?"
>
> "A Senator."
>
> "Better still. You're old enough now to grasp that there's no family without some skeleton or other in the cupboard, which the people concerned are terrified of

having discovered. The kids must be set hunting; it'll give them something to do. Family life as a rule is so boring! And then it'll teach them to observe, to look about them. It's quite simple. Those who contribute nothing will get nothing. When certain parents understand that they are in our hands, they'll pay a high price for our silence. What the deuce!—we have no intention of blackmailing them; we are honest folk. We merely want to have a hold on them. Their silence for ours. Let them keep silent and make other people keep silent, and then we'll keep silent too. Here's a health to them."

The antics of the young counterfeiters afford Gide an opportunity for some of his most brilliant passages, but it is what happened—or didn't happen—to Edouard which constitutes the action of the story. We come upon Edouard, the leading character of *The Counterfeiters,* at a moment when he has just discovered that he no longer has any romantic interest in Laura. Bernard Profitendieu falls in love with Laura, but his extreme youth and the circumstances under which he meets her—about to bear Vincent's child—render his devotion necessarily Platonic.

There is no romantic relationship between a man and a woman portrayed in the entire action of the book. The action hence lacks a dimension which one finds in the great fictions—even books which contain no female characters. "The youth" in *The Red Badge of Courage* will marry when he gets back from the war; in *Moby Dick* Ahab's quest for the White Whale leads him out of the every-day world of men and women—one reason why this quest is so dangerous. The world, whether we like it or not, is full of women. Edouard substitutes for his former love for Laura an incestuous attachment to his nephew, Olivier, but here again Gide's fatal double-mindedness, his inability to look at one side of a thing at a time, betrays him. Neither Edouard in his journal nor his creator in *his* journal ever recognizes the fact that incest and homosexuality are deviations from the normal pattern of conduct. Instead, Gide intimates that all would have been well if the couples had been paired off differently. Olivier's character would not have suffered the progressive blunting it does suffer if he had become the companion of his uncle rather than of the roué Passavant.

A study of Gide's play, *Oedipus,* sheds light on his novel. The Oedipus whom Gide invokes is not the Oedipus of mythology or Freudian theory. To this Oedipus the disasters of his family history are merely incidental to a greater misfortune—the failure, as it seems, to make man independent of the gods.

In Gide's play, Oedipus' sons, Eteocles and Polyneices, cherish an incestuous passion for their sister, Ismene. Their father is less concerned over this than over their apparent reluctance to subscribe to all his ideas. Sophocles, in contrast, is concerned with Oedipus' passions, not his ideas or opinions. One wonders whether a playwright can afford to treat incest as lightly as Gide does. The Princeton dowager who said that incest made her nervous was voicing the reactions of most of us. If we are not terrorized by the proximity of powerful, mysterious, and possibly destructive forces we are, at the least, made nervous by them, and it will be a sad day for the playwright—and novelist—if we become indifferent to them.

The primary aim of the fiction writer is to make his readers feel what a contemporary critic has called "primitive astonishments," and I do not know where the fiction maker is to find these astonishments if not in the family circle—that microcosm which, coming into being through the union, as it were, of two alien worlds, the masculine and feminine consciousnesses, constitutes an inexhaustible reservoir of drama, since it reflects the agonies and blisses resultant on the union of two lovers and the rebellions of sons and daughters against their fathers and mothers and the yearnings of fathers and mothers over their children, in an innumerable variety of complications. The playwright or novelist who neglects the drama inherent in these emotional complications does so at his own peril. In fiction, as in life, people are known by the company they keep: that is, are defined by their relations to other people.

A novelist is sometimes measured by his ability to set a number of characters in motion on his stage. In *The Counterfeiters* Gide's stage is crowded, but none of the characters is deeply explored and the interest in this and many of Gide's other novels is centered on the main character, who is absorbed in contemplating his own mirrored image.

Gide himself sums it up well when he says of Edouard, "He understands a great many things, but he is forever pursuing himself—through everyone and everything. Real devotion is impossible to him. He is a dabbler, a failure.

. . . A character all the more difficult to establish since I am lending him much of myself. . . ."

In his journal he also reports a conversation which he had with Roger Martin du Gard, whom he calls X:

> X maintains that a good novelist, before he begins to write his book, ought to know how it is going to finish. As for me, who let mine flow where it will, I consider that life never presents us with anything which may not be looked upon as a fresh starting point, no less than a termination. "Might be continued"—these are the words with which I should like to finish "The Counterfeiters."

He had his wish. The ending of *The Counterfeiters* is inconclusive. The complications introduced in the beginning are never resolved. The action, which on the surface is enormously complicated, does not so much mirror the stresses and strains, the cross-currents, of human life, as the confusions in the mind of the author. In short, it is Gide's own double-mindedness, his inability to make up his mind about anything, his penchant for attempting to look on two sides of one matter at the same time, that are his subject rather than anything that befalls his characters.

It is interesting and, I think, instructive, to compare Gide's work with that of another famous novelist, Marcel Proust. As a man, Proust, too, was beset with homosexual inclinations, but as an author Proust held to the normal viewpoint, that is to say, the viewpoint of heterosexuality. We may debate all we want to about whether Albertine was originally Albert but that is beside the point. We have the Duchesse de Guermantes, Madame Verdurin, Odette, Madame de Villeparisis; women, wives, widows, mistresses, sweethearts move through Proust's pages, companioned by the men with whom they are involved, giving Proust's work a dimension, an air of reality, which *The Counterfeiters,* for all Gide's mastery of style, all his brilliant insights, still lacks.

A further clue to Gide's tragedy—for his life strikes me as tragic—a further clue to his life and work may be found in an entry in his journal:

> Interrupted yesterday by a visit from X. His conversation upset me considerably. Have been reflecting a great deal on what X said. He knows nothing about my life but I gave him a long account of the plan of my Counterfeiters. His advice is always salutary because his point of view is different from mine. He is afraid that my work may be too factitious, that I am in danger of letting go the real subject for the shadow of the subject in my brain. What makes me uneasy is to feel that life (my life) at this juncture is parting company from my work, and my work is moving away from my life. But I couldn't say that to him. Up till now—as is right—my tastes, my feelings, my personal experiences have all gone to feed my writings; in my best contrived phrases I still feel the beating of my heart. But henceforth the link is broken between what I think and what I feel. And I wonder whether this impediment which prevents my heart from speaking is not the real cause that is driving my work into abstraction and artificiality. As I was reflecting on this, the meaning of the fable of Apollo and

> Daphne suddenly flashed upon me: happy, thought I, the man who can clasp in one and the same embrace the laurel and the object of his love.

The hero who does not reach out to a world outside himself—that world which, from time immemorial, has been personified in the feminine consciousness—is left confronting himself. The only adventure that beckons is self-expression. We are all of us, nowadays, vitally concerned with self-expression. That perhaps is why the heroes of so many modern novels are artists. As Mr. Blackmur put it, "The problem of the artist has become the problem of man."

The outstanding example of this kind of hero is, of course, Stephen Dedalus in James Joyce's *Portrait of the Artist as a Young Man.*[2] Joyce's story is based on a Greek myth, the story of Dedalus, who created the labyrinth in which King Minos of Crete confined the Minotaur and who equipped his son Icarus with wax wings for his flight over the seas. Joyce's hero has for surname the name of the pagan artificer but his given, or Christian, name is that of the first martyr, Saint Stephen. The Jesuits who have trained him think that he may take orders. The director calls him in one day to question him as to whether he has a vocation. Stephen listens to the director in "reverent silence."

> . . . through the words he heard even more distinctly a voice bidding him approach, offering him secret knowledge and secret power. . . .

But Stephen knows he will never become a priest:

> The voice of the director urging upon him the proud claims of the church and the mystery and power of the priestly office repeated itself idly in his memory. His soul was not there to hear and greet it . . . a definite and irrevocable act of his threatened to end forever in time and eternity, his freedom. . . . The snares of the world were its ways of sin. He would fall. He had not yet fallen but he would fall silently, in an instant. Not to fall was too hard, too hard. . . .

When he resists the call to a vocation he knows that it is forever, and as he walks back to his father's house after the conversation with the director he turns his eyes "coldly . . . towards the faded blue shrine of the Blessed Virgin. . . ." Like Icarus, Stephen is setting out on a journey with wings of wax. Though a believer—he never *loses* his faith, he *denies* it—he is an anti-Christ and has his precursor to make his way straight for him; he does not love any of his classmates and Cranly is the only one in whom he has confided. He has told Cranly all his sins and his soul-searchings. He asks himself:

> Why was it when he thought of Cranly he could never raise before his mind the entire image of his body but only the image of his head and face . . . the face of a severed head or death mask, crowned on the brows by its stiff black upright hair as by an iron crown?

He has a conversation with Cranly in which the way he is to go is revealed to him.

"It is a curious thing," Cranly says dispassionately, "how your mind is supersaturated with the religion in which you say you disbelieve. Did you believe in it when you were in school? I bet you did."

"I did," Stephen answers. And then: "I was someone else then."

"How someone else?" Cranly asks.

"I mean," says Stephen, "that I was not myself as I am now, as I had to become."

Cranly asks, "Do you love your mother?"

Stephen shakes his head slowly. "I don't know what your words mean," he says.

"Have you never loved anyone?" Cranly asks.

"Do you mean women?"

"I am not speaking of that," Cranly says. "I ask you if you ever felt love towards anyone or anything."

They are walking together and Stephen stares gloomily at the path. "I tried to love God," he says. "It seems now that I failed. It is very difficult. I tried to unite my will with the will of God instant by instant. In that I did not always fail. I could perhaps do that still. . . ."

The Christian theologians tell us that it is impossible to love God directly; we must love Him through His creatures, our fellow men. Stephen had tried to achieve the impossible. His sin, pride, begets in him a terrible restlessness. He is impelled to leave his home and college and seek a new life. His mother, as she puts his clothes in order, prays that in his own life, away from home and friends, he may learn what the heart is and what it feels, but Joyce has given us to understand that this will never happen.

Stephen has told Cranly that he is not afraid to make a mistake, "even a great mistake, a lifelong mistake and perhaps for eternity, too."

I suspect that Joyce's *Portrait* has been misread by a whole generation. It is not primarly, I think, a picture of the artist rebelling against constituted authority, but rather the picture of a soul that is being damned for time and eternity caught in the act of foreseeing and foreknowing its damnation. The passages I have just quoted throw considerable light on Joyce's intention. And we must take into consideration the fact that the action is based on the myth of Dedalus and Icarus. Joyce was a good classicist, steeped from youth in Greek mythology. He was not likely to base his action on a Greek myth without realizing its full implication; his imagination did not express itself in the kind of "modernistic" invention that characterizes, for instance, Jean Paul Sartre's play *The Flies* (*Les Mouches*). In that play, the Eumenides descend to the hero's level and after an unconvincing struggle follow him off the stage like whipped curs. But Joyce was more apt to attempt to plumb the fathomless depths that underlie every myth than to bring it up to date; in his works Furies remain Furies. The story follows the myth to its unhappy end. Stephen's father, who has the name of the old artificer Dedalus, is a man of the nineteenth century. His skepticism and materialism, Joyce shows us, have helped to construct the labyrinth from which both he and his son are trying to escape. Dedalus the father escapes through his love of his fellow men. Stephen goes with his father to visit his father's college and is amazed at his father's love for his old cronies; there was not one of his set, Simon Dedalus tells his son, who did not have some talent, some merit that lifted him above the ordinary.

We are reminded of Leigh Hunt's "Abou Ben Adhem." Abou, as you may recall, awoke one night and saw an Angel "within the moonlight in his room." The Angel was writing in a book of gold "the names of those who love the Lord." Ben Adhem asked, "And is mine one?" The Angel answered, "Nay, not so," and Abou said, "I pray thee, then, write me as one that loves his fellow men." The poem ends:

> The Angel wrote, and vanished. The next night
> It came again with a great wakening light,
> And showed the names whom love of God had blessed
> And lo! Ben Adhem's name led all the rest!

Leigh Hunt has chosen an Angel whose theology—like that of some modern novelists when they choose to enter the field—seems a little weak, but apparently the Angel has been straightened out by its second visit. Not so Stephen Dedalus. Unlike Abou Ben Adhem and his father Simon, Stephen himself feels that his own heart is as "cold as the craters of the moon." The only one of his classmates with whom he is intimate is Cranly, and they are intimate only because Cranly feels an almost scientific curiosity about the working of Stephen's mind. The father Dedalus, through love for his fellow men, escapes from the trap which his own hands have built—or rather his mind!—as Dedalus of old escaped. But Dedalus' son Icarus flew too near the sun. The wings that his father made for him were of wax. They melted under the sun's fierce heat and he fell into the sea.

Stephen Dedalus towers high among heroes. His sin is the same as Lucifer's. He said what Lucifer said: "I will not serve," and he falls from a great height, as Lucifer fell, from pride.

Today there is another hero of self-expression, one who does not assert himself as Stephen does or, unlike Sartre's Mathieu Delarue, attempt to evade existence—who is, rather, bent on expressing himself through sacrifice. Our age is not characterized, on the whole, by religious orthodoxy, but the Christ figure is remarkably prevalent in contemporary fiction. Faulkner's corporal in *A Fable,* Robert Jordan in Hemingway's *For Whom the Bell Tolls,* Scott Fitzgerald's Dick Diver in *Tender Is the Night,* and his *Gatsby*—all seem bent on laying down their lives to find something better. Even Thomas Wolfe's hero in *You Can't Go Home Again,* writing his farewell letter to Foxhall Edwards, hopes to "leave this life for greater living."

A man or woman who attempts to model a life on that of Christ is indeed a noble subject for fiction. It is disconcerting—at least to this reader—to find that some of our most talented novelists do not always do their best work when attempting to portray such a subject. Albert Camus' brilliant novel *The Fall* (*La Chute*) is a case in point. The novel has a strong theological bias, having for its subject the depravity inherent in all of us since the Fall of Man. It is full of profound religious symbolism. The hero has chosen to live in Amsterdam, of all cities, because it is almost wholly surrounded by water. Everywhere water appears as the symbol of the infinite, and this world, at the last, is characterized as " a vast holy water font." M. Camus has a real gift for writing fiction and is, besides, technically accomplished. In his story the complication of the action progresses beautifully and with seeming inevitability toward its resolution—but the action is never resolved. M. Camus perhaps taxes his reader's credulity too roughly at the very moment when the reader should be taking everything the author tells him on faith; his hero advances a modernistic and highly individualistic interpretation of the Crucifixion, which arouses wonder and speculation rather than belief: he holds that as a result of Herod's Slaughter of the Innocents Christ developed a guilt complex so enormous that He could rid Himself of it only by forcing the Jews and Romans to crucify Him. A little research into the "vital statistics" of the times might have dispelled this curious delusion. In ancient times the number of Herod's victims was supposed to be great; the Byzantine liturgy speaks of 14,000, the Syrian menologies, 64,000, and an "accommodation" of certain verses of the Apocalypse puts it at 144,000. But modern hagiographers, beginning with Bishop Butler, point out that Bethlehem was a small place and, even when its environs were included, could not have produced more than twenty-five boy babies under two years of age, at the very most. Some authorities place the number as low as half a dozen. A guilt complex as enormous as that which M. Camus' hero ascribes to the Savior of the World would seem to call for the slaughter of considerably more innocents than history —or hagiography—gives us reason to believe in.

William Faulkner's recent novel, *A Fable,* is another example of a book which is marred by its author's misconception of or failure properly to explore his subject matter. The book is, on the whole, ill-written. The sentences are almost all of the same length and have few of the subtle modulations which play such an important part in his finest rhetorical flights. More serious still, his scenes often lack the lifelikeness which in many of his other works almost takes the reader's breath away. In *A Fable* Faulkner has a Roman Catholic priest say, "It wasn't He with His humility and pity and sacrifice that converted the world; it was pagan and bloody Rome which did it with His martyrdom; furious and intractable dreamers had been bringing that same dream out of Asia Minor for three hundred years until at last one found a caesar foolish enough to crucify Him . . . because only Rome could have done it, accomplish it, and even He . . . knew it, felt and sensed this, furious and intractable dreamer though He was. Because He even said it Himself: On this *rock* I found my *Church,* even while He didn't—and never would—realize the true significance of what He was saying, believing still that He was speaking poetic metaphor, synonym, parable—that *rock* meant unstable, inconstant heart, and *Church* meant airy faith."

Christian theologians, for all their differences, generally agree on one thing: the uniqueness of the Christian scheme of redemption—the uniqueness being that a god sacrifices himself instead of being torn to pieces by his crazed followers, as with Dionysos Zagreus, for instance. As Freud remarked in *Totem and Taboo:* "We are much disturbed by the spectacle of a youthful god sacrificing himself, but let us pass that over."

One does not need formal training in theology to write novels, but a novelist is bound by the nature of his medium to know enough about any subject he treats to achieve the illusion of lifelikeness, of verisimilitude, whether the subject be plumbing, nuclear physics, millinery, or the habits of baseball players or courtesans. A novelist who has chosen a nuclear physicist or a medical doctor for his hero will doubtless engage in considerable research before he tries to tell the story of such a man's life. Emile Zola, for instance, prepared himself for his description of Nana's death by getting detailed reports from experts. He wrote to one of them, "I have received your book on smallpox. Evidently it will do for my description. . . . I am very much tempted to make it black smallpox, which, in point of horror, is the most original. Only I will confess that if you could manage to see a corpse of a person who died of this disease . . . what a nice little job!—you would oblige me greatly. In that way I should not have to invent anything—I should have a real death-mask. Be sure to dwell at length on the state of the eyes, of the nose, and of the mouth. . . ."

The novelist who has for his hero a Christ-like figure would do well to acquaint himself with the outlines of the life of the historical personage known as Jesus Christ before writing his novel—or he may wind up with a plot that he cannot resolve. And the resolution of the complications which he himself has set in motion is the foremost concern of a novelist. Anthony Trollope once asked his readers to decide how one of his novels should end, even leaving it to the reader to say whether or not the heroine should marry the hero. Henry James was so shocked at this evasion of responsibility that he called it "a betrayal of the sacred calling." A novelist, he held, is a historian, with a responsibility as great as that of "a Macaulay or a Gibbon." Certainly a man who undertakes to write a novel undertakes to contrive the illusion of a universe, and it is well for him to know as much as possible about the workings of that universe before he attempts to order it.

Chapter Twelve

Reading for Enjoyment

T. S. Eliot, a good many years ago, made one of those pronouncements that cause the serried ranks of his admirers to bow in the wind like a field of ripe wheat—as he himself once put it. It is possible, he said, that the novel may be dead as an art form.

Mr. Eliot would not make such a suggestion without good reason. It is well, however, when considering the novel to keep in mind the fact that it differs from all other mediums. It is more intimately concerned with the conduct of life itself than any other art form. The nature of the medium is so peculiar that even such a bold and subtle critic as Mr. Eliot may have been deceived as to its condition, may have mistaken—shall we say?—sleep or a comatose condition for death.

But Mr. Eliot's intuitions are not to be lightly disregarded. It is apparent that something *is* wrong, but I am not convinced that his is the right answer. For one thing, the novel has hardly had time to attain maturity as an art form; from Fielding's day to Faulkner's is not more than two hundred years, a period of time that could be spanned by the consecutive lives of three men. The novel is, perhaps, if we permit ourselves to use the figure, not the child strangled in the cradle—the fate which Baudelaire, another bold and subtle critic, prophesied for the world when it shall have become wholly mechanized—but rather a backward child, or a child who may have taken the wrong turn on the path it was appointed to follow—more than one wrong turn perhaps.

Some critics maintain that one of the wrong turns is the present misconception of the role of the hero, the preoccupation with self-expression, with being rather than doing, which is characteristic of many modern novelists. The comparison of Fielding's *Tom Jones* with some present-day novels supports such a view. Fielding, if he were alive today, might not accept Mathieu Delarue, for instance, as the hero of a novel for the simple reason that Mathieu was not in love with either Marcelle or Ivich.

In *Tom Jones* the reader's attention is centered on the love affair between Tom and Sophia Western but there is a great deal else going on. The passion of love is only the "core" of the action of this novel. For a passion, once unleashed, has a way of unleashing other passions—a principle adhered to as firmly by the police force of any large modern city as by the Greek tragedians.

There is, indeed, no passion to which the human soul is subject that is not fit for fiction, as Chekhov once pointed out to a lady admirer who objected to some passages in his short stories because of what she considered their immorality. When we are tempted to censure an author because the characters in his novels do not adhere to our own code of morals we ought to remind ourselves that some of the greatest heroes of fiction—indeed of myth and legend—trespassed against the accepted code of their day. Prometheus brought fire from heaven against the express commands of his gods. Very unpleasant things happened to him in consequence; Aeschylus and the writers who came after him go to considerable lengths to see to it that their readers realize what Prometheus suffered. Suffering is one of the tasks appointed a hero. The reader who prefers that nothing happen to the characters in a novel that he wouldn't want to happen to himself is depriving himself of a vital experience. The whole Western World would be poorer if Aeschylus had felt that the eagle's tearing of Prometheus' liver was too unpleasant to contemplate, or if Sophocles had been too squeamish to let Oedipus put his own eyes out with the brooch torn from his dead wife's dress.

As for the reader who does not see why a novel cannot concern itself primarily with ideas rather than action: he, I think, fails to take into consideration that the concern of a novel is life, and that life means action. Thought, certainly, is a form of action, but the one of all others that is least easily dramatized. No matter how intelligent we ourselves are, as readers we are always more interested in what a character in a novel does than in what he thinks. All great novelists know this instinctively. As Proust[1] put it, "A book in which there are theories is like an article from which the price mark has not been removed."

But perhaps this question may be more easily answered by the consideration of a brilliant contemporary novel in which ideas and opinions predominate over action. Aldous Huxley's *After Many a Summer Dies the Swan* is a case in point. An American millionaire, who is determined not only never to die but to remain young and vigorous forever, is taken to visit the fifth Earl of Gonister, who, having the same desire, had subjected himself some years before to certain scientific experiments. The Earl and a female companion who has undergone the same treatment are found in a deep cellar beneath the Earl's family mansion disporting themselves in a manner which now recommends itself to them as both seemly and pleasant. The American millionaire is horrified, both by their appearance and by their simian antics, but when the scientist who brought him there asks if he still wants to undergo the treatment himself, he replies that he does, "for they seem to be having a good time—in their own way." It is one of the most entertaining pieces of contemporary writing, but neither the Earl of Gonister nor the American millionaire seems to me to qualify as the hero—or villain—of a novel. They are too unambitious, too much R. P. Blackmur's "hero of self-expression," incapable of the adventures that befall real heroes—or villains—since all their energies are absorbed in being—or not being—instead of in doing.

Perhaps the belief that it is possible to have a "novel of ideas" is part of a trend that is prevalent today: the inclination toward the shortcut as being not only time-saving but actually desirable in itself, as evidenced by the widespread demand for compact formulations of various kinds of knowledge which it often takes a lifetime to acquire. Mr. Huxley writes a beautiful, lucid prose and burns with some of the same fervor that animated his grandfather, the biologist Thomas Huxley. His disapproval of both the Earl of Gonister and the American millionaire is evident in every word he writes and what he has to say is morally bracing, but his book does not deal with the conduct of life in the way that Dickens or Thackeray or Stendhal or any of the great novelists deals with life. His characters tend to pale in the rarefied intellectual atmosphere in which they move. The reader knows as soon as they come on the scene what the author thinks of them and consequently has no difficulty in making up his own mind about them. But Dostoevski's characters, or Tolstoi's, or Henry James', come toward us, as it were, out of a fog of creation. We have to observe them a while before we have any idea of what they are about. It may be years before we make up our mind whether they behaved well or ill in a given situation.

There remains the reader who, like William James, feels that the author ought to write books that people want to read rather than the books he himself feels impelled to write. This argument is not new. Indeed, it has been advanced wherever and whenever readers have concerned themselves seriously with the art of fiction. R. G. Collingwood, the British philosopher whom I quoted earlier, would hold, I think, that this question and the others I have cited are all included in the argument started by Socrates and continued by Plato and Aristotle as to the distinction between "amusement art" and "art proper," a distinction which he feels is just as important today as it was in the time of the ancients.

The reader who demands that his own moral code shall not be infringed upon, or his feelings lacerated by any unpleasant happenings in any book he reads, is actually demanding that the emotions aroused in him by the reading of any work of art shall not overflow into real life but shall be "earthed"—and not far from his easy chair. He asks only to be entertained by the reading of this or that book. He does not want to be made a better man as the result of reading it. He is like a person who prefers to picnic at the foot of a mountain and forgo the view he would get from the summit rather than undergo the rigors of the climb to the top. There is, of course, no compulsion on any of us to make us climb mountains if we do not feel like it. Indeed, there are days when it would be inadvisable, even foolhardy, to attempt the climb.

Still, if we never stir about we may eventually lose the use of our legs. If we spend all our time picnicking in the valley we may come to feel that there is nothing worth seeing outside of it, may be tempted to dismiss as vain imaginings the wonders that our more energetic friends tell us they have viewed from the mountaintop and, losing touch with reality, become prisoners of our own inanition.

I suspect that this is the plight of many modern readers of fiction. There is no harm in the contemplation of "make-believe" situations. Indeed, such contemplation may be salutary under the right circumstances. The danger sets in when people get so in the habit of discharging their emotions upon make-believe situations that they come to think of emotion as something that can be excited and enjoyed for its own sake, without reckoning with any of its practical consequences. The person who does not reckon with the practical consequences of his emotions often finds himself in unpleasant predicaments, as our workhouses and penitentiaries abundantly testify. A society in which there is a preponderance of members who habitually do not reckon with the practical consequences that follow upon emotion is in danger of its existence. The "bread and circuses" which kept the Roman populace quiet were, perhaps, symptoms of the disease to which that society finally succumbed.

It is possible that the same disease is endemic among ourselves. We have a greater craving to be amused than our fathers and grandfathers had and the past twenty-five years have shown an unprecedented growth in the number of vehicles of popular amusement. In addition to the legitimate stage, the radio and the cinema and in the last few years television compete for our attention. These amusements not only are offered to occupants of the easy chair but actually invade the classroom. The high-school student who is directed by his teacher to read a certain novel as often as not goes to see a film version of the story, or, if it has not been filmed, hastens to the nearest stationer, who, if the book in question is well enough known, furnishes him with a summary or condensation of its action. And this practice is not confined to young people in the secondary schools. There are today "children's versions" or condensations of almost all the books in which children two generations ago delighted—from the Grimms' *Fairy Tales* to *Gulliver's Travels.*

On the other hand, people—even people who own television sets—continue to read novels. And while novelists may not have as many readers as they once had they may have better readers. The schoolboy whose grandfather read Scott, Dickens, Thackeray, and George Eliot for pleasure may find on the shelf, alongside the condensations that will save him the exertion of reading the works of these writers, inexpensive editions of the works of even greater writers of whom his grandfather never heard. And the works of these great writers are every day more widely distributed. Nowadays it is hard to find a college student who has not read at least one novel by Tolstoi or Dostoevski or Stendhal. And our own great master, Henry James—who, as we have seen, did not have a single discerning reader in his lifetime—now has the kind of reading every writer longs for; not only are his works widely distributed but for the past fifteen or twenty years some of the finest critical minds on both sides of the Atlantic (but more particularly on this side) have devoted their best efforts to their explication.

The novel, as I have pointed out, has had a comparatively short history as an art form. Nevertheless, the genius of the fiction writer has manifested itself in a variety of ways during this period. In the space of a little over two hundred years we have had novelists whose work bears the marks of greatness differing from one another as much as, say, Hawthorne and Hemingway.

Sometimes a novelist's strength seems to lie in the fact that he "speaks" for his times. Balzac, I suspect, was such a novelist, and so was Dickens. Readers of their works were charmed to see, as if reflected in a mirror, the mysterious currents of human thought and emotion which they themselves were swayed by. Dickens—even when, as in *Bleak House* or *Oliver Twist,* he is waging war against social injustice—is speaking for and to people of his own day, and people listened to him so well that he had the joy of seeing the child-labor laws in England reformed, to a great extent as the result of his writings. Such writers often have another gift which appeals powerfully to the imagination: the faculty of crystallizing in the reader's mind ideas, opinions, even emotions, of which the reader himself was only half aware.

There are other great writers who are not read properly in their own day for the reason, perhaps, that their readers are not yet born. What they have to say to their own generation is said so at cross-purposes and with such apparent irrelevance that it is not understood. They are, as it were, giants who tower above their own age to cast their shadows across the next. Hawthorne was such a writer, and Flaubert, and Henry James.

But all of these great writers, whether they find their audience among friends and neighbors or address figures that are dim because they are shrouded in the mists of the future, join hands across time and space, I think, in Melville's "shock of recognition." And all of them offer the reader the same thing. It is best summed up, perhaps, under the title of "enjoyment"—enjoyment as opposed to amusement.

Mr. Collingwood defines amusement as "enjoyment which is had without paying for it. Or rather, without paying for it in cash." Amusement, he maintains, is always "put down in the bill and has to be paid for later on."

> For example [he writes], I get a certain amount of fun out of writing this book. But I pay for it as I get it in wretched drudgery when the book goes badly, in seeing the long summer days vanish one by one past my window unused, in knowing that there will be proofs to correct and index to make, and at the end black looks from people whose toes I am treading on. If I knock off and lie in the garden for a day and read Dorothy Sayers, I get fun out of that too; but there is nothing to pay. There is only a bill run up, which is handed in next day when I get back to my book with that Monday-morning feeling. . . . I may get back to the book feeling fresh and energetic, with my staleness gone. In that case my day turned out to be not amusement but recreation. The difference between them consists in the debit or credit effect they produce on the emotional energy available for practical life.

This example might be drawn from the life of any professional writer. The novelist who offers his readers "enjoyment" rather than "amusement" may find in it some consolation. His sales are certain to be small. If he is in a state of unusual dejection over his last royalty report he might find it heartening to visit any large book store or the circulation desk of any library and observe the procession of well-dressed women—American men, alas, seldom read novels!—all of whom are intent on procuring a copy of the same novel: a novel that they have been told they *must* read, usually one whose appeal is based on the unreal picture it gives of life. The novelist whom I have imagined as observing this scene, veiled in his anonymity—

like Dr. Johnson standing behind his screen because his coat was too shabby and spotted for him to receive the condescensions of the Earl of Chesterfield out in the open—may be pardoned if the curiosity that is so vital a part of every novelist's make-up impels him to cast searching glances at the countenances under the becoming hats, in an effort to ascertain which of these readers is seeking a little wholesome amusement (which she can well afford) or which one is simply adding another item to a bill, now long overdue, which in all probability she will never be able to pay.

But if the searching glance which an author, from time to time, turns upon the long procession of readers lights upon the countenance of a reader who is concerned not with amusement but with enjoyment, the author himself feels a joy so transcendent that he is impelled, as it were, to stretch out a hand and to draw the reader after him into that great dance in which genius, in all countries, all ages, foots it featly.

For the reader, too, has his role to play. There is indeed a moment in the creation of any work of art when reader and author are assigned the same role. We are all of us in the same situation with respect to life as it really is. Baudelaire pictured it in his famous sonnet in which his hero, Man, wandering through a "forest of symbols" comes upon a temple whose "living pillars" observe him with "familiar looks." His task is to find out what these living pillars are saying to him. It is only by interpreting the "confused words" that breathe from them that he can find his way—that is, find out where he is, and, even more important, *who* he is.

Another great writer—a Frenchman, too—has come to the same conclusion about life and art. Marcel, the hero of Proust's long sequence of novels, as a child once woke at midnight "not knowing where I was" and not "at first who I was."

> . . . But then the memory, not yet of the place in which I was, but of various other places where I had lived, and now might very possibly be, would come like a rope let down from heaven to draw me up out of the abyss of not-being, from which I could never have escaped by myself: in a flash I would traverse and surmount centuries of civilisation, and out of a half-visualised succession of oil-lamps, followed by shirts with turned-down collars, would put together by degrees the component parts of my ego.

Proust's hero's long search for himself—or for the "lost time" that holds his true identity—begins one afternoon when, "weary after a dull day with the prospect of a depressing morrow," he, contrary to his usual custom, accepts a cup of tea from his mother and then soaks one of the little cakes called *petites madeleines* in it. An exquisite pleasure invades his senses at the taste of the crumbs soaked in hot tea, a pleasure which turns into a joy so powerful that it makes him indifferent to the vicissitudes of life. He realizes that this "all-powerful joy" is connected with the taste of tea and cake, but he realizes, too, that it infinitely transcends those savors and he asks himself, "Whence did it come? What did it signify? How could I seize upon and define it?"

Proust concludes that truth is recorded in our consciousness by associations with objects outside ourselves:

> The sight of the cover of a book one has previously read retains, woven into the letters of its title, the moonbeams of a far-off summer night. The fragrance of the morning cup of coffee brings us that vague hope of fair weather which so often in former years smiled at us . . . as we drank our coffee from a bowl of creamy white china, crinkled like coagulated milk. An hour is not merely an hour. It is a vase filled with perfumes, sounds . . . and climates.

Everything that we have ever seen or heard or smelled or tasted constitutes a passage in the book of memory, a book that is written not in letters but in "signs." Proust says:

> To read the subjective book of these strange signs . . . is a creative act. . . . This book, the most difficult of all to decipher, is also the only one dictated to us by reality, the only one the "imprinting" of which on our consciousness was done by reality itself. . . . The ideas formed by pure intellect have only a logical truth, a potential truth; the selection of them is an arbitrary act. The book written in symbolic characters not traced by us is our only book. . . .
>
> I perceived that, to describe these impressions, to write that essential book, the only true book, a great writer does

> not need to invent it, in the current sense of the term, since it already exists in each one of us, but merely to translate it. The duty and the task of a writer are those of translator. . . . The grandeur of real art . . . is to rediscover, grasp again and lay before us that reality from which we live so far removed and from which we become more and more separated as the formal knowledge which we substitute for it grows in thickness and imperviousness—that reality which there is grave danger we might die without ever having known and yet which is simply our life, life as it really is, life disclosed at last and made clear, consequently the only life that is really lived, that life which in one sense is to be found at every moment in every man, as well as in the artist. . . .

The truth of our own lives is written in the lives—and the looks—of others. "To see ourselves as others see us" is always a rewarding experience even if it is sometimes trying. And we can learn from imaginary companions as well as from the people we meet and talk with every day. A young woman may find out as much about her own character and probable destiny from contemplating the life of Tolstoi's Anna Karenina as from sessions with her psychiatrist—and possibly even more. A young man who, for a while, has Dostoevski's Prince Myshkin as his imaginary companion may discover months or years after he has read the book that he has capabilities for extraordinary endeavor that he had not thought himself to possess. A brilliant young fiction writer of my acquaintance said after reading Stephen Crane's *Red Badge of Courage,* "I didn't make much of it when I read it—but two days later I gave a long shudder." His shudder registered, I suppose, the impact of the Civil War on his consciousness, an impact, to this sensitive person, as sharp, as dramatic as that made by the war of which he himself was a veteran.

A work of fiction, a novel, does not always transport us to a battlefield. It may take us to a palace, an island in the South Seas, a country about which we know nothing but its glamorous name. A book—a well-composed book—is a magic carpet on which we are wafted to a world that we cannot enter in any other way. Yet, in another sense, all true works of fiction have their scenes laid in the same country, and the events take place in the same climate: that country, that climate which we all long for and in our several ways strive to reach—the region where truth is eternal and man immortal and flowers never fade.

The reader who prefers enjoyment to amusement and the author who realizes that it is his duty to provide it have the same lifelong preoccupation. Each bends over the great, flowing stream of human consciousness, intent on deciphering the characters of his "only book." There is a peculiar pleasure in store for each: the moment when they realize that they are, after all, engaged in the same task—when they salute each other in the shock of recognition.

Notes

Chapter One

1. "The myth about Plato's banishing the artist (or poet) from his ideal city is derived from a misunderstanding of the *Republic*: 'We should reverence him as something holy and marvellous and delightful: we should tell him that there is not any one like him in our city—and there is not allowed to be; and we should anoint him with myrrh and crown him with a diadem and send him away to another city, and for our own part employ for our welfare's sake a drier and less amusing poet and story-teller, who should represent to us the discourse of a good man.' . . . The misinterpreters of Plato assure us that the victim of this banishment is the poet as such. If they had read the sentence to the end as I have quoted it, they would have seen that he could not be that; he must be some one kind of poet; and if they had remembered what went before, they would realize what kind of poet he was: not even the representative poet as such, but the entertainer who (admittedly with marvellous skill and very amusingly) represents trivial or disgusting things." —R. G. Collingwood, *The Principles of Art* (New York: Oxford University Press, 1938).
2. *Letters of Sherwood Anderson,* edited by Howard Mumford Jones and Walter Rideout (Boston: Little, Brown, 1953).

Chapter Two

1. *Art and Scholasticism,* by Jacques Maritain; translated by J. F. Scanlan (New York: Charles Scribner's Sons, 1930).
2. Flaubert proved this when he wrote *A Simple Heart,* the story of a simple servant woman to whom, apparently, nothing out of the way ever happened but whose life nevertheless moved to a triumphant conclusion.

Chapter Three

1. Aristotle in the *Poetics* defines a tragedy as the "imitation of an action that is serious and also, as having magnitude, complete in itself; in language with pleasurable accessories, each kind brought in separately in the parts of the work; in a dramatic, not a narrative form; with incidents arousing pity and fear, wherewith to accomplish its catharsis of such emotions."
2. Quotations are from the translation of *Oedipus Rex* by Dudley Fitts and Robert Fitzgerald (New York: Harcourt, Brace and Co., 1949). The translators' spellings are used in the quotations. The commentary uses the common spellings, for example, Jocasta for the translators' Iocastê.

Chapter Four

1. All quotations of *Madame Bovary* are from the translation by Eleanor Marx Aveling (New York: Modern Library).
2. Quotations of *The Idiot* are from Constance Garnett's translation (New York: Macmillan, 1920).

Chapter Five

1. *The Craft of Fiction,* by Percy Lubbock (New York: Viking Press, 1957 [reissue]).
2. The reader who wishes to know more of Richardson's technique would do well to read Ford Madox Ford's discussion of the work of Richardson and Fielding in his brilliant, uneven, and much-neglected *The March of Literature* (New York: Dial Press, 1938).
3. The quotations are from Louise and Aylmer Maude's translation of *War and Peace* (New York: Simon and Schuster, 1942).
4. The quotations are from C. K. Scott-Moncrieff's translation of *La Chartreuse de Parme,* by Stendhal (Marie-Henri Beyle) (New York: Boni and Liveright, 1925).
5. All quotations from the *Iliad* are from Richmond Lattimore's translation (Chicago: University of Chicago Press, 1951).

Chapter Six

1. Some of this discussion is taken from *The House of Fiction* by Caroline Gordon and Allen Tate (New York, Charles Scribner's Sons, 1950). Quotations from Hemingway's "Today Is Friday" are from *The Short Stories of Ernest Hemingway* (New York: Charles Scribner's Sons, 1954).
2. When Bertrand Russell ascribed the virtues of his prose style to the fact that he was privately educated, T. S. Eliot, with unusual acerbity, remarked on what a misfortune it was for the western world that Earl Russell had not in his youth been subjected to any formal disciplines. Mr.

Faulkner's admirers may perhaps be pardoned if they arrive at the conclusion that it is a great misfortune for contemporary fiction that Mr. Faulkner did not receive a classical education. An even casual acquaintance with what the Greeks called the "middle diction" (exemplified in the works of Sophocles as opposed to those of Aeschylus on the one hand and Euripides on the other) might prevent his lapsing into bathos in his efforts to portray for us the great mythological figures which haunt his imagination.

Chapter Seven

1. Quotations on pages 111-14 are taken from E. M. Forster's *Aspects of the Novel* (New York: Harcourt, Brace and Co., 1927).
2. *The Method of Henry James,* by Joseph Warren Beach (New Haven: Yale University Press, 1918; enlarged edition with corrections, Philadelphia: Albert Saifer, 1955).

Chapter Eight

1. *The Notebooks of Henry James,* edited by F. O. Matthiessen and Kenneth B. Murdock (New York: Oxford University Press, 1947).
2. *The Art of the Novel,* by Henry James; edited by R. P. Blackmur (New York: Charles Scribner's Sons, 1935).

Chapter Nine

1. This and the following quotations concerning the elder Henry James are from *New England Saints,* by Austin

Warren (Ann Arbor, Michigan: University of Michigan Press, 1956).

2. *English Prose Style,* by Herbert Read (New York: Pantheon, 1952).
3. From *Dubliners,* in *The Portable James Joyce* (New York: Viking Press, 1947).
4. From *Anima Poetae* selections, in *The Portable Coleridge* (New York: Viking Press, 1950).

Chapter Ten

1. *Age of Reason* by Jean Paul Sartre; translated from the French by Eric Sutton (New York: Knopf, 1947).

Chapter Eleven

1. *In Defense of Reason,* by Yvor Winters (New York: Swallow-Morrow, 1946).
2. Much of the discussion of Joyce's *Portrait of the Artist* is taken from an article in the *Sewanee Review* (summer 1953) by Caroline Gordon. Quotations from *Portrait of the Artist* are from the Viking Compass edition.

Chapter Twelve

1. The quotations are from C. K. Scott-Moncrieff's translation of Marcel Proust's *Remembrance of Things Past* (New York: Modern Library).

Index

"Abou Ben Adhem" (Leigh Hunt), 214
Across the River and into the Trees (Ernest Hemingway), 100
Action, 18, 30, 59, 68, 76, 85, 87, 89, 90, 113, 145, 194, 197, 222
Aeschylus (525-456 B.C.), 25, 56, 127, 222, 238
After Many a Summer Dies the Swan (Aldous Huxley), 222-24
Age of Reason (Jean Paul Sartre), 180-90, 215, 221, 239
A la Recherche du temps perdu, see Remembrance of Things Past
Alice's Adventures in Wonderland (Lewis Carroll), 60
Ambassadors, The (Henry James), 117-18, 120, 129, 132-42, 143, 154-55
American, The (Henry James), 122
"Amusement art," 11-12, 224, 228, 229, 230, 234
Ancient Mariner, see Rime of . . .
Anderson, Sherwood (1876-1941), 15, 235
Anna Karenina (Leo Tolstoi), 233
Arabian Nights Entertainments, The, 75
Aristotle (384-322 B.C.), 12, 26-27, 143, 224, 236; definitions by, of: discovery, 31; metaphor, 163; Peripety, 31; tragedy, 194, 236
Art and Scholasticism (Jacques Maritain), 17, 235
"Artists in residence," 8
Art of the Novel, The (Henry James), 125-26, 238
"Art proper," 11-12, 224
As I Lay Dying (William Faulkner), 76, 103
Aspects of the Novel (E. M. Forster), 112, 238
Austen, Jane (1775-1817), 160-61
Authority, 73, 93, 105
Autobiography of Alice B. Toklas, The (Gertrude Stein), 195-96
Aveling, Eleanor Marx, 236

Balzac, Honoré de (1799-1850), 62, 64, 121-22, 227
Baudelaire, Charles (1821-1867), 66, 164-66, 220, 230
Beach, Joseph Warren (1880-1957), 115-17, 118, 119, 125, 238
Beardsley, M. C., 19-20
Beauvoir, Simone de, 182
Beyle, Marie-Henri, *see* Stendhal
Bible, 159, 162
Blackmur, Richard P., 190-91, 223, 238
Bleak House (Charles Dickens), 90-91, 228
Boccaccio, Giovanni (1313?-1375), 75
Böhme, Jakob (1575-1624), 5
Boon, the Mind of the Race (H. G. Wells), 111-12

Bostonians, The (Henry James), 153
Brontë, Emily (1818-1848), 161-62
Brooks, Van Wyck, 114
Butler, Bishop Joseph (1692-1752), 216

Callimachus (b. 330? B.C.), 5
Cambridge History of English Literature (George Sampson), 77-78
Campbell, Joseph, 189
Camus, Albert, 215-17
Canterbury Tales, The (Geoffrey Chaucer), 75
Carlyle, Thomas (1795-1881), 193
Carroll, Lewis (Charles Lutwidge Dodgson) (1832-1898), 60, 168-70
Cary, Joyce (1888-1957), 98, 100, 110
Catiline (Lucius Sergius Catilina) (c. 108-62 B.C.), 149
Center of vision, 72-73, 81, 93, 103, 105, 125
Central intelligence, 120-44
Chandler, Raymond Thornton, 19
Charterhouse of Parma, The (Stendhal), 91-92, 237
Chartreuse de Parme, La, see Charterhouse of Parma
Chaucer, Geoffrey (c. 1343-1400), 75
Chekhov, Anton Pavlovich (1860-1904), 221
Chesterfield, Philip Dormer Stanhope, 4th Earl of (1694-1773), 230
Chesterton, Gilbert Keith (1874-1936), 14, 15
Christ as symbol, 101, 215, 218
Christmas Holiday (Somerset Maugham), 117-18
Cicero, Marcus Tullius (106-43 B.C.), 149
Cimabue, Giovanni (d. 1302?), 142
Clarissa (Samuel Richardson), 79-81
Coleridge, Samuel Taylor (1772-1834), 69, 74-75, 128, 157-58
Collingwood, R. G., 10-12, 26, 224, 228, 235
Complication, 26, 27, 29, 30-31, 35, 52, 53, 165, 216, 219
"Composition of scene," 61-62, 64, 71
Conrad, Joseph (1857-1924), 96
"Constants" in fiction, 24-25
Controlling image, 164
"Correspondances" (Charles Baudelaire), 164-66, 230-31
Counterfeiters, The (André Gide), 196-209
Cowley, Malcolm, 17-18
Craft of Fiction, The (Percy Lubbock), 79-81, 120, 142, 237
Crane, Harold Hart (1899-1932), 201
Crane, Stephen (1871-1900), 91-93, 97, 205, 233

Daisy Miller (Henry James), 122, 153
"Dead, The" (James Joyce), 68, 156, 164, 166
Death in Venice (Thomas Mann), 195
Decameron (Boccaccio), 75
Defoe, Daniel (1659-1731), 98, 160, 162, 163
Dickens, Charles (1812-1870), 4, 14, 15, 89-91, 120, 224, 227, 228
Dictionary of Modern English Usage (H. W. Fowler), 32
Dionysos Zagreus, 218
Discourse, novel as, 81
"Discovery," 31, 37
Dostoevski, Fëdor Mikhailovich (1821-1881), 20, 23, 69-71, 224, 227, 233
Doyle, Sir Arthur Conan (1859-1930), 11
Dramatic method, 117, 118, 131, 132, 143
Dr. Grimshawe's Secret (Nathaniel Hawthorne), 166-67
Dubliners (James Joyce), 155-56, 239

INDEX

Duccio di Buoninsegna (1278-1319), 142
Du Gard, Roger Martin, 208
Dunne, Finley Peter (1867-1936), 6
Dupee, F. W., 122

Edel, Leon, 121
Effaced narrator, 124
Eliot, George (Mary Ann Evans) (1819-1880), 227
Eliot, Thomas Stearns, 220, 237
Emerson, Ralph Waldo (1803-1882), 192
English Prose Style (Herbert Read), 152-54, 157-62, 239
"Enjoyment art," 228, 229, 230, 234
"Entertainments," 12
Euripides (480?-406 B.C.), 56, 238
Existentialism, 180, 183, 215
"Extrapolation," 60

Fable, A (William Faulkner), 215, 217
"Fallacy of Imitative Form, The," 193-94, 196
Fall, The (Albert Camus), 215-17
"Fall of the House of Usher, The" (Edgar Allan Poe), 30
Farewell to Arms, A (Ernest Hemingway), 99-100
Faulkner, William, 5, 76, 102-104, 149, 215, 217, 220, 237
Faux Monnayeurs, Les, see Counterfeiters
Fielding, Henry (1701-1754), 77, 81, 82, 119, 131, 159, 171-80, 220, 221, 237
"Figure in the Carpet, The" (Henry James), 115
Fitts, Dudley, 236
Fitzgerald, Francis Scott Key (1896-1940), 12, 21, 215
Fitzgerald, Robert, 236
Flaubert, Gustave (1821-1880), 21-22, 64, 66, 104, 105, 148, 166, 228, 236
Flies, The (Jean Paul Sartre), 213
Ford, Ford Madox (original surname Hueffer) (1873-1939), 145-46, 237
Forster, Edward Morgan, 81, 112, 133-34, 141, 238
For Whom the Bell Tolls (Ernest Hemingway), 215
"Four questions": what, to whom, when, where, 58-59
Fowler, Henry Watson (1858-1933), 32
Freud, Sigmund (1856-1939), 218
Freudian critics, 148
Fuller, Sarah Margaret (1810-1850), 193

Gainsborough, Thomas (1727-1788), 68
Garnett, Constance, 236
Genesis, Book of, 61
Gide, André Paul Guillaume (1869-1951), 196-210
Giotto di Bondone (c. 1266-c. 1337), 142
Golden Bowl, The (Henry James), 112-14, 120, 122, 132, 144
Good Soldier, The (Ford Madox Ford), 145-46
Gordon, Caroline, 237, 239
Gothic romance, 166
Goya y Lucientes, Francisco Jose de (1746-1828), 68
Grady, Henry Woodfin (1850-1889), 149
Great Gatsby, The (F. Scott Fitzgerald), 215
Greene, Graham, 12
Grimms' *Fairy Tales,* 226
Gulliver's Travels (Jonathan Swift), 158-59, 226
Guy Domville (Henry James), 123

Hamlet, The (William Faulkner), 102-103
Harris, Joel Chandler (1848-1908), 75

Hawthorne, Nathaniel (1804-1864), 23, 166-68, 192, 227, 228
Hemingway, Ernest, 62, 78, 99-100, 101-102, 146-47, 215, 227, 237
"Heracleidae, The," 194
Hero: artist as, 190, 210; decline of, 171-191; Prometheus as, 221; qualifications of, 171-73, 178, 189, 191, 210, 223, 230
"Hero as Disconsolate Chimera, The" (R. P. Blackmur), 190-91
Herself Surprised (Joyce Cary), 98
Hesiod (eighth century B.C.), 74
History of Tom Jones, a Foundling, The (Henry Fielding), 81, 171-80, 183, 189-90, 221
Holmes, Sherlock, 11
Homer, 74, 93-94, 103-105, 194, 237
Horace (Quintus Horatius Flaccus) (65-8 B.C.), 5
House of Fiction, The (Caroline Gordon and Allen Tate), 237
Hubris, 28, 29, 40, 55
Hunt, James Henry Leigh (1784-1859), 214
Huxley, Aldous Leonard, 10, 222-24
Huxley, Thomas Henry (1825-1895), 223
Huysmans, Joris-Karl (1848-1907), 4

Ideas, novel of, 9-10, 223
Idiot, The (Fëdor Dostoevski), 23, 69-71, 233, 236
Iliad (Homer), 74, 93-94, 103, 105, 237
"I'm a Fool" (Sherwood Anderson), 16
Immediacy, 110
In Defense of Reason (Yvor Winters), 239
"Intentional Fallacy, The," 19-20
Irony, 32-33, 35, 51, 53
"I Want to Know Why" (Sherwood Anderson), 16

"Jabberwocky," *see Through the Looking Glass*
James, Henry (1843-1916), 6, 7, 22, 54, 56, 81, 89, 104, 110, 111-19, 120-44, 149, 154-55, 157, 162-64, 166, 167-68, 219, 224, 227, 228; "compositional law," 120, 125; "divine principle of scenario," 120, 124; dramatic method, 117; "exquisite scheme," 115-16; "figure at the window," 125-29; Freudian critics of, 148; "later method," 103, 118, 123, 125, 128, 131, 153; use of metaphor, 163; "Papa's ideas," 148-49; technical discoveries, 120, 125, 127, 130, 143
James, Henry, Sr. (1811-1882), 148-52, 153-54, 238
James, William (1842-1910), 6, 7, 8, 10, 123, 150-51
Jemima Puddle-Duck (Beatrix Potter), 25, 49-55
Jesperson, Otto (1860-1943), 152
Johnson, Samuel (1709-1784), 163, 230
Jones, Howard Mumford, 15, 235
Jones, Tom, see History of Tom Jones
Journals of André Gide (trans. Justin O'Brien), 197-98, 206, 208-210
Joyce, James Augustine Aloysius (1882-1941), 5, 18, 68, 69, 81, 99, 155-56, 164, 166, 192, 210-14, 239

Kafka, Franz (1883-1924), 5
Kenton, Edna, 122
Kierkegaard, Sören Aabye (1813-1855), 5, 6

Lattimore, Richmond, 237
Leavis, F. R., 112-14
Lewis, Clive Staples, 60
Lewis, Harry Sinclair (1885-1951), 20

Lubbock, Percy, 22, 72, 79-81, 120, 129, 142, 237

Madame Bovary (Gustave Flaubert), 22, 64-67, 68, 105-110, 236
"Make-believe" situations, 225
Mann, Thomas (1875-1955), 195
March of Literature, The (Ford Madox Ford), 237
Maritain, Jacques, 17, 122
Matthiessen, Francis Otto (1902-1951), 238
Maude, Louise and Aylmer, 237
Maugham, William Somerset, 117-18
Maupassant, Guy de (1850-1893), 116
Melville, Herman (1819-1891), 24, 205, 228
Metaphor, 163, 164, 165, 166, 168
Method of Henry James, The (Joseph Warren Beach), 115-17, 118-19, 238
"Middle diction," 238
"Misther Dooley" (Finley Peter Dunne), 7
Moby Dick (Herman Melville), 205
Moll Flanders, The Fortunes and Misfortunes of (Daniel Defoe), 98
Mouches, Les, see Flies
Murdock, Kenneth B., 238

Nana (Émile Zola), 218
Narrative method, 72, 90, 117, 119, 131, 132, 143, 159-60
Narrator: first-person, 76, 78, 95, 97-100, 102-103, 106, 110, 120, 129; omniscient, 49, 53, 82, 86, 89, 91, 94, 120, 129; third-person, 53, 76, 91, 94-95, 100
Naturalism, 164
New England Saints (Austin Warren), 149-52, 238-39
Nietzsche, Friedrich Wilhelm (1844-1900), 197
Notebooks of Henry James, The (ed. F. O. Matthiessen and Kenneth B. Murdock), 120, 123-24, 130, 153, 238
Notes of a Son and Brother (Henry James), 148-49
Novel, essential nature of, 13, 14, 16-17, 18, 72, 110, 131, 197, 220

Odyssey (Homer), 194
Oedipus (André Gide), 206
Oedipus Rex (Sophocles), 25, 26-52, 222, 236
O'Hara, John Henry, 62, 104
Oliver Twist (Charles Dickens), 4, 228

Pamela; or Virtue Rewarded (Samuel Richardson), 78
Panoramic method, 83, 85-86, 89, 91
Paragraph, 156-57
Père Goriot (Honoré de Balzac), 62-64
Peripety, 31, 32
Persuasion (Jane Austen), 160-61
"Plane of action," 81
Plato (427?-347? B.C.), 12, 224, 235
Poe, Edgar Allan (1809-1849), 30
Poetics (Aristotle), 26, 143, 194, 236
Portrait of a Lady, The (Henry James), 125
Portrait of the Artist as a Young Man, A (James Joyce), 18, 155, 210-14, 239
Possessed, The (Fëdor Dostoevski), 20
Potter, Beatrix (1866-1943), 25, 49, 52
Principles of Art, The (R. G. Collingwood), 11, 228-29, 235
Prometheus, 221-22
Protagonist, 28
Proust, Marcel (1871-1922), 20, 208-209, 222, 231-33, 239
"Psychological" literary critics, 6

Read, Sir Herbert Edward, 152-54, 157-62, 163, 239

Reality, 192-93, 196, 225
Red and the Black, The (Stendhal), 91
Red Badge of Courage, The: An Episode of the American Civil War (Stephen Crane), 91-93, 205, 233-34
Remembrance of Things Past (Marcel Proust), 208-209, 222, 231-33, 239
"Representative art," 12
Republic (Plato), 12, 235
Resolution, 26, 27, 30-31, 35, 52, 53, 54, 165, 216, 219
Richardson, Samuel (1689-1761), 77-82, 99, 131, 237
Rideout, Walter, 235
Rime of the Ancient Mariner, The (Samuel Taylor Coleridge), 74-75, 97
Rodker, John, 145
Russell, Bertrand, 237
Saddest Story, The, see Good Soldier, The

Sampson, George, 77-78
Sartre, Jean Paul, 180-90, 213, 215, 221, 239
Sayers, Dorothy, 229
Scanlan, J. F., 235
Scarlet Letter, The (Nathaniel Hawthorne), 23
Scenic method, 14, 83, 85, 90, 91, 94, 118, 129
Science fiction, 60, 69
Scott, Sir Walter (1771-1832), 116, 119, 227
Scott-Moncrieff, C. K., 237, 239
Second Sex, The (Simone de Beauvoir), 182
Sentence, 152, 154-56, 168, 217
Septimius Felton (Nathaniel Hawthorne), 166
Sewanee Review, 19, 239
"Shock of recognition," 24-25, 64, 121, 228, 234
Short Stories of Ernest Hemingway, The, 237
"Sibling rivalry," 6
Simple Heart, A (Gustave Flaubert), 104, 148, 236
Society, the Redeemed Form of Man: An Earnest of God's Providence (Henry James, Sr.), 150
Socrates (469-399 B.C.), 224
Sophocles (495-406 B.C.), 25, 30, 31, 32, 47, 48, 49, 56, 143, 206, 222, 236, 238
Sound and the Fury, The (William Faulkner), 102, 103
Specification, 54, 56, 89
"Spotted Horses" (William Faulkner), 104
Stein, Gertrude (1874-1946), 15, 192-93, 195
Stendhal (Marie-Henri Beyle) (1783-1842), 91-92, 224, 227, 237
Sterne, Laurence (1713-1768), 159
"Stream of consciousness," 81
Style, 143-44, 145-70
Sun Also Rises, The (Ernest Hemingway), 78, 147
Supernatural, 28, 100, 166
"Suspension of disbelief," 69
Sutton, Eric, 239
Swift, Jonathan (1667-1745), 60, 158-60, 162, 163, 164, 226
Symbolism, 164, 165
"System of observation," 22, 24

Tate, Allen, 237
"Telling" method, 117-18, 124-25
Tender Is the Night (F. Scott Fitzgerald), 215
Thackeray, William Makepeace (1811-1863), 15, 87-91, 117, 171, 224, 227
"Three-dimensionalism," 104
Three Lives (Gertrude Stein), 195
Through the Looking-Glass (Lewis Carroll), 168-70
"Today is Friday" (Ernest Hemingway), 100-102, 237

Tolstoi, Count Leo (Lev Nikolaevich) (1828-1910), 11, 19, 21, 23, 83-87, 89, 224, 227, 233
Tom Jones, see History of Tom Jones
Tone, 145-70
Totem and Taboo (Sigmund Freud), 218
"Triumph of the Egg, The" (Sherwood Anderson), 16
Trollope, Anthony (1815-1882), 219
Turgenev, Ivan Sergeëvich (1818-1883), 21
Twentieth Century Novel, The (Joseph Warren Beach), 117-19

Ulysses (James Joyce), 18, 81
Uncle Remus stories (Joel Chandler Harris), 75
Unities: of place, time and action, 56, 58, 71; of action, 160; of place, 57; of space, 61; of time, 61

Vanity Fair (William Makepeace Thackeray), 87-89
Verisimilitude, 124-25, 142, 166, 217, 218, 219, 222
Victoria, Queen, as creation of Richardson, 78
Viewpoint, 53, 71, 72, 73-74, 82, 86, 91, 94-95, 106, 107

War and Peace (Leo Tolstoi), 11, 19, 23, 83-87
Warren, Austin, 149-52, 238-39
Warren, Robert Penn, 81
Wells, Herbert George (1866-1946), 60, 111-12, 117
West, Rebecca (Cicily Isabel Fairfield), 114
Whitehead, Alfred North (1861-1947), 6
Whitman, Walt (1819-1892), 192
Wilson, Edmund, 24
Wimsatt, W. K., Jr., 19-20
Wings of the Dove, The (Henry James), 120, 132, 144
Winters, Arthur Yvor, 193-94, 239
Wolfe, Thomas Clayton (1900-1938), 21-22, 194, 215
"Written," 148
Wuthering Heights (Emily Brontë), 161-62

Yeats, William Butler (1865-1939), 154
You Can't Go Home Again (Thomas Wolfe), 215

Zola, Émile (1840-1902), 22, 218